Employment Security in a Free Economy

Work in America Institute's National Policy Studies

With the publication in fall 1984 of Work in America Institute's newest national policy study, *Employment Security in a Free Economy*, the Institute will have completed its fifth major study since January 1978. Previous studies are:

> *Job Strategies for Urban Youth: Sixteen Pilot Programs for Action*
> *The Future of Older Workers in America*
> *New Work Schedules for a Changing Society*
> *Productivity through Work Innovations*

A companion volume to *Employment Security in a Free Economy* is *Employment Security in Action: Strategies That Work* by Jocelyn F. Gutchess, another in the Pergamon Press/ Work in America Institute Series.

All of the above books are available from Pergamon Press, Inc.

About Work in America Institute

Work in America Institute, Inc., a nonprofit, nonpartisan organization, was founded in 1975 to advance productivity and the quality of working life. It has a broad base of support from business, unions, government agencies, universities, and foundations, as reflected in its board of directors, academic advisory committee, and roster of sponsoring organizations.

Through a series of policy studies, education and training programs, an extensive information resource, and a broad range of publications, the Institute has focused on the greater effectiveness of organizations through the improved use of human resources.

Employment Security in a Free Economy

A Work in America Institute Policy Study

Directed by Jerome M. Rosow, President
and Robert Zager, Vice-President
for Policy Studies and Technical Assistance

Pergamon Press
New York • Oxford • Toronto • Sydney • Paris • Frankfurt

Pergamon Press Offices:

U.S.A.   Pergamon Press Inc.. Maxwell House. Fairview Park.
                     Elmsford. New York 10523. U.S.A.

U.K.   Pergamon Press Ltd.. Headington Hill Hall.
                     Oxford OX3 0BW. England

CANADA   Pergamon Press Canada Ltd.. Suite 104. 150 Consumers Road.
                     Willowdale. Ontario M2J 1P9. Canada

AUSTRALIA   Pergamon Press (Aust.) Pty. Ltd.. P.O. Box 544.
                     Potts Point. NSW 2011. Australia

FRANCE   Pergamon Press SARL. 24 rue des Ecoles.
                     75240 Paris. Cedex 05. France

FEDERAL REPUBLIC Pergamon Press GmbH. Hammerweg 6
OF GERMANY   6242 Kronberg/Taunus. Federal Republic of Germany

Library of Congress Cataloging in Publication Data
Work in America Institute.
    Employment security in a free economy.

    (A Work in America Institute policy study)
    Includes index.
    1. Job security--United States. I. Rosow, Jerome M.
II. Zager, Robert. III. Title. IV. Series.
ISBN 0-08-030975-5

Printed in the United States of America

Contents

In the opinion of the Board of Directors of Work in America Institute, *Employment Security in a Free Economy* is a timely, balanced review of a crucial problem in the U.S. economy. Its recommendations are practical and deserve careful study by decision makers in every sector.

Clark Kerr

CLARK KERR
Chairman
Work in America Institute

Preface

Employment Security in a Free Economy, the report of Work in America Institute's fifth national policy study, addresses a problem that is fundamental to the most effective use of human resources—employment security. It is an issue that must be dealt with constructively and imaginatively if we are to meet the competitive challenges of the coming decades.

This study's objective is to provide decision makers in business, unions, and government with a battery of workable alternatives for achieving greater stability in the work force. It advocates, not a guarantee of lifetime employment with one employer or permanent rights to a job, but a steadily growing opportunity for employees to continue in gainful employment, preferably within the same organization, for as long as they wish. Employment security is seen, not as an impediment, but as a spur to corporate prosperity.

Many managers believe that business crises and economic reverses inevitably result in large-scale personnel dismissals. However, corporate policies can be put into place which anticipate economic pressures and respond in a variety of ways. These policies treat personnel dismissals as a last rather than a first option and recognize that preserving the skill, knowledge, talent, and loyalty of a highly trained and experienced work force is critical to the long-term growth and survival of the enterprise.

Corporations that have embraced these policies—among them the strongest and most productive in America—have found that employment security releases the creative energies and ideas of employees. Resistance to change is replaced by an openness to challenge, narrow rivalries by teamwork—responses that offer the enterprise a clear competitive advantage over companies operating in the conventional mode.

We believe that this report casts new light on the subject of employment security and points the way toward positive action on a large scale by organizations of all kinds. The approaches and programs it suggests, and its 26 practical recommendations, are directed toward all sectors of the economy, but particularly toward employers.

The study—and a companion book of cases, *Employment Security in Action: Strategies That Work* by Jocelyn F. Gutchess, to appear in the spring of 1985—have been supported by grants from the Andrew W. Mellon Foundation, the Charles Stewart Mott Foundation and, for European coverage, The German Marshall Fund of the United States. The statements made and views expressed, however, are solely the responsibility of Work in America Institute. Both findings and recommendations have the approval of the Board of Directors of Work in America Institute, acting through its chairman, Dr. Clark Kerr.

The successful completion of this policy study would not have been possible without the aid of the following:

☐ The members of our outstanding National Advisory Committee, whose names are listed in these pages. (Their participation, however, does not necessarily imply agreement with the findings and recommendations of the report.)

☐ Paul E. Barton, for his paper on "Skill-Development Alternatives to Layoffs and Income Maintenance"

☐ Fred Best, for his paper on "Short-Time Compensation in North America: Trends and Prospects"

☐ Professor Irving Bluestone, for his paper on "Approaches to Employment Security—A Union View"

☐ John F. Donnelly, for his paper on "Strategies and Tactics Leading to Employment Security"

☐ Professor Fred K. Foulkes and Anne Whitman, for their paper on "Full Employment, Product/Marketing Strategies, and Other Considerations"

☐ Jocelyn F. Gutchess, for her paper on "Subcontracting and Other Employment-Buffering Policies"

☐ Professor Robert W. Keidel, for his paper on "Intercompany Loans of Surplus Employees: A Critical Perspective"

☐ Claire Kolmodin, for her paper on "Employment Security at Control Data Corporation"

☐ Wilbur J. Rowland and Al Christner, for their paper on the "Buick Employe Development Center"

☐ Freda Rutherford, for her paper on "Downriver Community Conference." (Also Abt Associates, for permission to reproduce parts of their reports on the experience of the Downriver Community Conference.)

☐ Professor Yoshi Tsurumi and Rebecca R. Tsurumi, for their paper on "A New Mechanism of Employment Adjustment for the U.S."

☐ Hans Ursing, for materials on Trygghetsradet, the Swedish Employment Security Council

☐ Dan L. Ward, for his paper on "The Cost Implications of a No-Layoff Policy"

☐ Howard O. Williams, for his paper on "Outplacement as a Means of Employment Security"

☐ Tom Wood, for his paper on "Toward a National Policy on Retirement Age"

We wish to acknowledge also the invaluable assistance of the following staff members of Work in America Institute: Beatrice Walfish, editorial director; Frances Harte, managing editor; Joan White, senior production assistant; Stephanie McDowell, production assistant; Virginia Lentini, assistant to the vice-president for policy studies; Ellen Daniels, information service manager; Cynthia Rubino, information specialist; and Linda Calabrese, library information assistant.

We are especially appreciative of the devoted and creative efforts of Robert Zager, vice president for policy studies, for the direction of the entire study.

Jerome M. Rosow
July 1984

Summary/Recommendations

Employment security has become the top priority of American labor unions. In seeking security at the bargaining table, unions are giving voice to the felt needs of nonunion as well as union employees, of managers and supervisors as well as the rank and file.

Employers are uncertain how to respond to these demands. Although they understand that employees feel insecure, they believe that in a free economy management must be free to lay people off or dismiss them when necessary. They also have the erroneous notion that people can find another job if they really try and that income maintenance programs, such as unemployment insurance, are sufficient to sustain them during the job search.

This report argues that increasing the security of employees can serve to raise the performance of an organization without diminishing its freedom. Employers must continually change products, technology, production processes, marketing, and relations with customers, suppliers, shareholders, and employees. To do so, they need the cooperation of their employees, but employees will welcome change only if they feel secure in their jobs. They are bound to resist change, overtly or covertly, as long as the danger of job loss hovers in the background.

THE CASE FOR EMPLOYMENT SECURITY

The fact that employment security opens the door to rapid technological change and productivity improvement was demonstrated as long ago as the first quarter of the nineteenth century, when the English industrial pioneer, Robert Owen, used it to convert a rundown Scottish cotton mill into a world-famous enterprise.

In the United States, several dozen companies of varied sizes and industries, including many household names, have been known to follow Owen's no-layoff policy. Some have done so for decades. Others have begun within the past five years.

It is not uncommon for a firm to maintain a no-layoff policy for a while and then abandon it, usually during a general economic recession, and this is often cited as proof that employment security is risky. What it really proves is that a blanket no-layoff policy, guaranteeing continued employment regardless of what happens outside the firm, is risky. But employment security should not be so narrowly defined: We view it, rather, as flexible, evolutionary, and open-ended.

Employment Security as a Continuum

This report defines employment security as a continuum rather than a single fixed point. In a given organization, its extent is measured by the degree to which employees are assured that, regardless of internal or external changes, they will continue in employment as long as they live up to the terms and conditions of employment. Within that definition, an infinite number of variations may exist, depending on such factors as different classes of employees, permanent or temporary status, length of service, types of changes covered, aspects of the job that are protected, quid pro quos, duration of guarantee, and whether employment may be continued in another firm.

The phrase, "job security" is avoided because it often implies a right to cling to a particular job, no matter what. Employment security is distinguished from income security in that the former is concerned with continuation of employment, while the latter has to do with what happens in the absence of employment.

A Microeconomic Focus

The focus of this report is microeconomic; namely, it addresses what employers, employees, and unions could do to ensure that people currently employed continue in employment, and what government could do to support these programs. The report deals only indirectly with macroeconomic issues, such as full employment and national industrial policy, which require separate study. However, we do recommend major changes in federal policies that advance the welfare of employers but disregard the security of employees.

Although employment security is in the interest of both employer and employees, pressure for it originates mainly from organized labor at the bargaining table. Union members have put employment security at the head of the agenda because they predominate in industries hardest hit by deregulation and competition. Nonunion employees feel the same urgency but lack a voice. The pressures will build as the effects of deregulation and competition intensify and spread.

In recent years scores of unions have traded wages, benefits, and work rules for employment security. Farsighted employers will look beyond the immediate test of strength implied in these bargains and perceive a more durable lesson: that employees are willing to give up a lot and contribute more for the sake of career employment. Employment security thus holds great potential for raising the level of employee commitment to the firm and for reinforcing the shared goals of employer and employee.

In Europe, the reluctance of employers to provide employment security led to restrictive legislation on layoffs and plant closings. In the United States, there have been numerous proposals for state and federal legislation on advance notice of plant closings. But American employers dislike legislative rigidities as much as American workers dislike Japanese-style checks on their freedom to change employers. The best way to keep the federal government out of employment security is for employers to pre-empt the field by setting an example of enlightened corporate action. While no single employer or small number of employers can change the system, many major employers acting in concert could.

Employment Security vs. Employment at Will

The U.S. economy operates under a system of employment at will, combined with unemployment insurance and other income security devices. This system does not and cannot elicit employee commitment to continual change because employees do not believe the system will protect them adequately if their employers decide they have become surplus to the company's needs.

Some 70 million nonunion employees in the United States can

be fired at any time for any cause, or for no cause. Union members and people with statutory protection (women, minorities, handicapped people) cannot be dismissed arbitrarily, but they can be laid off or dismissed whenever any change in the business makes them surplus. The typical union contract lays down *procedures* for layoff or dismissal; it does not otherwise circumscribe the employer's freedom.

The income security system is inadequate because: (1) many displaced workers are unable to find a suitable new job and so remain unemployed for a long time; (2) unemployment insurance benefits keep a family from starving but provide a relatively low standard of living; (3) women and minorities are especially vulnerable because they cannot acquire enough seniority to establish a foothold; (4) older workers find it almost impossible to obtain a new job at a level comparable to the one they have left; (5) loss of employment in the United States means a loss of social status; (6) physical and mental health deteriorate badly during unemployment, and the costs of caring for them are borne by employers, in the form of taxes and charitable donations.

Employment security not only avoids the disadvantages of income security but offers important advantages of its own. In the long run, enlightened employers will prefer it because it:

☐ Induces employees to support continual change and thereby makes for a more competitive company.

☐ Encourages employers to invest in training and developing people.

☐ Helps managers, supervisors, and workers to concentrate on the common goal: success of the enterprise.

☐ Enhances the employer's image in the community.

☐ Enables the employer to move rapidly when a business slump ends.

☐ Reduces the cost of turnover.

☐ Preserves skills and maintains productivity.

☐ Avoids the costs of "bumping" and related turmoil.

☐ Avoids the costs of income security.

☐ Avoids the costs of replacing people who leave in a layoff.

THE COMMITMENT TO EMPLOYMENT SECURITY

An employer who decides to make employment security a cornerstone of corporate strategy will want to provide enough security to elicit employee support, but not so much as to endanger the enterprise.

Employees understand that employers cannot have complete control over business conditions, nor realistically guarantee continued employment, regardless of the circumstances. What they seek is assurance that the employer will (1) fully protect them against harm from actions that *do* lie within the employer's control, and (2) make every effort to protect them from harm due to events beyond the employer's control.

Employment security policies can be tailored to suit such commonsense expectations. They can begin modestly and expand by discrete steps in accordance with stated goals and timetables. To have the desired effect, however, these policies must be clearly understood by employer, employees, and unions.

Recommendation 1: In view of the clear net-cost advantage to employees and employer, we strongly recommend that employers guarantee that no permanent employee will be laid off or downgraded due to any labor surplus arising from internal corporate productivity/performance changes.

Recommendation 2: After balancing the benefits and costs of layoffs and dismissals against those of available alternatives, employers should issue the broadest commitment they can afford with respect to employment security during periods of business decline. They should also declare their intention to broaden the coverage as business success permits, creating an incentive for productivity. In addition, employers should promise that if sacrifices become necessary, they will be shared equitably across the organization.

Recommendation 3: Employers should make a written commitment that, in the event that economic recessions make dismissals unavoidable, they will actively assist dismissed employees to find suitable new jobs with other firms.

THE NEED FOR PLANNING AHEAD

A pledge of employment security can prove extremely costly if it is not backed by careful planning. Fortunately, every major change of circumstances that may threaten security can be foreseen by the employer long before its impact. It is feasible, therefore, to have plans ready in advance. The sooner that managers, employees, and unions are involved in planning and action, the greater the chances are of containing threats to employment security.

The likelihood that plans will be made and acted upon in due time depends on (1) the authority vested in the planners, and (2) the weight actually assigned by the employer to employment security as an element in appraising managerial performance.

Recommendation 4: Employers should institute a system of planning human-resource needs and deployments as an integral part of the corporate business planning process.

Recommendation 5: Primary responsibility for human-resource planning should be fixed at the highest level of the firm, but all managers should be responsible for detailed human-resource plans in their own areas.

Recommendation 6: Since every significant challenge to employment security can be anticipated far in advance, employers should use this period to ensure that their responses are ready to execute at the appropriate time.

Recommendation 7: On all matters affecting employment security, the CEO should regularly consult with senior local and international officers of the union and should invite the union as early as possible to join in designing and executing responsive measures.

LEAN STAFFING

Employment security is continually jeopardized by the natural tendency of employers to let the work force grow faster than the work load. Imbalances can be avoided by adopting policies and programs that avoid the creation of surpluses in the first place. The four principal lines of attack are (1) linking long-term work-load plans to authorized work-force levels to ensure that protected employees do not exceed the number necessary for long-term growth of the work load; (2) devising careful hiring and firing practices to ensure a competent work force; (3) drawing up annual operating plans that meet short-term fluctuations of work load without adding protected employees; and (4) adopting production, marketing, and financial policies that minimize sudden changes in the size of the protected work force.

Recommendation 8: Since the accumulation of surplus employees in prosperous times can undermine management efforts to maintain employment security in hard times, employers should ensure that (1) authorized work-force levels are tied to long-term work-load plans; (2) employees are competent to meet the changing needs of the organization; (3) annual operating plans can accommodate short-term increases of work load without adding protected employees; and (4) production, marketing, and financial policies help to avoid sudden changes in work-force levels.

Recommendation 9: Every work unit in an organization should establish, by agreement with top management, tough but realistic staffing standards. If the work unit wants to add employees in excess of the standard, it should have to obtain top management permission. Adherence to standard is facilitated if (1) all new hires are regarded as career employees; (2) all protected employees are, by agreement, willing and able to be deployed in a wide variety of assignments; (3) unsatisfactory performers are brought up to standard, reassigned, or dismissed early in their careers.

Recommendation 10: "Buffers"—such as overtime, transfers of people or work load, temporary employees, and subcontracting—can help greatly in maintaining employment security in the face of short-term business fluctuations. At the same time, buffers may cause unwanted side-effects. Employers should, therefore, use them in accordance with clear ground rules agreed upon with employees and local and international unions.

Recommendation 11: Firms seeking to stabilize their work loads for the sake of employment security should focus on (1) stabilizing the flow of orders, (2) maintaining growth at a sustainable rate, (3) avoiding overdependency on a single market or customer, and (4) achieving flexibility in the use of production personnel, plant, process, and materials.

RESPONDING TO TEMPORARY ECONOMIC DECLINES

Temporary economic declines are usually seasonal, cyclical, or occasional; generally last no longer than six months; and are not necessarily related to the economy as a whole. A commitment to employment security implies that in such a decline employers will defer layoffs as long as possible through a variety of approaches.

One approach is to restrict hiring and take advantage of attrition. Another is to try to sustain the work load of protected employees by releasing temporary employees, bringing subcontracted work in-house, assigning employees to lower-priority work, and increasing marketing efforts. One particularly desirable use of "downtime" in a slump is intensive training and retraining.

If, despite having tried these approaches, an employer still finds it necessary to lower payroll costs, work sharing is often more advantageous than layoffs. Work-sharing—the voluntary reduction of paid working hours for all instead of total loss of work time for some—is in the best interests of employer, employees, and unions. However, unemployment insurance laws in most states discourage its use.

Recommendation 12: As soon as employers detect the approach of a temporary decline in demand for their products or services, they should update and set in motion plans for (1) restricting hiring, (2) retrieving from temporary employees or subcontractors any work that can reasonably be done in-house, (3) expanding the demand for output, and (4) assigning surplus employees to lower-priority work.

Recommendation 13: If a temporary decline in demand makes it essential to cut payroll costs faster than restricted hiring alone can do, the company, its employees, and its unions should jointly work out arrangements for temporarily reducing either wage and salary rates or the number of paid working hours. All stakeholders in the firm should share equitably in the hardship.

Recommendation 14: To employees faced with layoffs, the employer should offer the alternative of remaining on the payroll and being paid the equivalent of unemployment insurance benefits while taking part in training and education programs approved by the employer.

Recommendation 15: Before instituting layoffs, the employer should make it clear to employees and unions that no better solution was available.

RESPONDING TO PERMANENT DECLINES
OF WORK LOAD

Contrary to popular belief, a permanent loss of work load—whether due to technological obsolescence, marketing shifts, or intensified competition—need not preclude the possibility of employment security.

The first response to such a loss should be to attempt to replace the lost work load by tapping new sources: subcontracting for other firms, introducing new products, establishing subsidiaries, and bringing previously subcontracted work back in-house.

Should that approach fail, the employer may seek ways of reducing wage costs without dismissals by restricting hiring and taking advantage of attrition, work sharing, early retirement, and productivity programs—the latter undertaken in cooperation with the union, if one is present.

If, in fact, dismissals are unavoidable, the company can still help displaced employees obtain suitable work in other organizations through training and outplacement. It can also offer financial and professional assistance—and sometimes subcontracts—to employees who are interested in self-employment. Another course open to employers is to create new jobs through the sale of the business, conversion of the physical facilities of the plant, and/or efforts to attract small employers to the area.

Recommendation 16: Employers intent on honoring a commitment to employment security should not be deterred by the permanent decline of demand for part or all of their output. In cooperation with their employees and unions, they should make every effort to replace the lost work load, reduce costs without dismissals and, if all else fails, help dismissed employees find suitable work elsewhere.

Recommendation 17: In its efforts to offset permanently lost demand, the employer should, after retrieving from temporary employees and subcontractors work that can be done in-house, consider launching new products or services, acquiring or creating subsidiaries, or accepting subcontracts from other firms.

Recommendation 18: If it becomes necessary to reduce payroll costs permanently, the employer should first try to do so without dismissals, using such methods as restricted hiring, work sharing, early retirement, phased retirement, wage reductions, and intensive productivity-raising programs.

Recommendation 19: If the dismissal of protected employees becomes unavoidable, the employer should actively help them find suitable work elsewhere. The employer can provide financial bridging, pension portability, outplacement services, or retraining for those seeking new jobs; professional and financial assistance and subcontracts for those preferring self-employment. If the area suffers from a shortage of suitable jobs, the employer should do as much as possible to create or attract replacement jobs.

ALLIANCES

Employers and unions faced with the prospect of imminent dismissals often cannot muster the energy, know-how, or resources to meet a commitment to employment security. Many of the difficulties can be resolved through ad-hoc alliances with other employers and unions, with local and state governments, and with educational institutions. Existing alliances, such as area labor-management committees, can be adapted to these uses.

Such groups in the United States and Europe have achieved notable results in outplacement, retraining, and job creation. Of these programs, the most widely applicable is outplacement, but its potential is stunted by the absence of job banks acceptable to employers.

Recommendation 20: Employers and local and international unions in a metropolitan area or a major industrial region should band together to organize a computer-based job clearinghouse and keep it up to date. Where an area labor-management committee already exists, it should take an active part in this effort.

Recommendation 21: Regional groups of employers and unions, both local and international, should form alliances to provide retraining and education for employees who have lost jobs through no fault of their own. To gain flexibility and economy, the allies should avail themselves of the services of postsecondary schools.

Recommendation 22: Employers, local and international unions, and local and state governments should form alliances to diversify the job base in areas where employment depends heavily on the fortunes of a single industry or a few firms. They should try to attract small firms that (1) demonstrate potential for growth, (2) are industrially diverse and have economic cycles that differ from those that prevail in the area, and (3) find a large part of their market at a safe distance from the work site. Alliances should also include those union-management pension funds over whose investment policies the unions exercise some control. Such funds have billions of dollars in assets and would like to invest a portion in ventures to create jobs for union members. Governments should assist by enabling pension funds to make such investments, subject to limited gains and limited risks.

A SUPPORTIVE ROLE FOR GOVERNMENT

Federal laws and regulations, with a few exceptions, such as the Job Training Partnership Act, either ignore or discourage the practice of employment security. Federal actions are also responsible for economic recessions, which undermine the employment security policies of even the strongest companies.

The government can begin to reverse these disincentives by assisting employers who try to fulfill their commitments to employees and by requiring employers who receive federal largesse to provide an appropriate measure of employment security.

One way of assisting employers who are committed to employment security has been devised by several states: passage of short-time compensation (STC) laws, which alter unemployment compensation regulations to make work sharing a more attractive alternative to layoff. This strategy has been reinforced by federal legislation and is spreading to additional states, but not nearly fast enough.

Recommendation 23: We recommend that Congress establish a more rational balance between capital mobility and employment security, through the following actions:

1. Federal tax policy should be redefined to recognize the fundamental rights of every citizen to tax protection against economic hardship, such as unemployment. Further, tax policy should treat individuals and families with a more reasonable degree of equity as compared to corporations.

2. When employers seek favorable tax treatment in a merger,

acquisition, or leveraged buyout, they should be required to show that they have provided appropriately for the security of regular employees who, through no fault of their own, have been downgraded or made surplus as a result of the transaction.

3. Employers should be allowed to take tax write-offs and credits against future income (a) for expenses incurred in keeping surplus employees on the payroll during a temporary business decline, and (b) for expenses incurred in helping dismissed employees retrain for, obtain, and relocate to new jobs. Employees dismissed without fault should be allowed tax credits against future income for (a) earnings and benefits lost between dismissal and reemployment, (b) any decrease of earnings and benefits between old and new jobs, and (c) costs incurred in retraining for, obtaining, and relocating to a new job.

4. When employers seek import protection or export subsidies, they should be required to show that they have provided appropriately for the security of regular employees who, through no fault of their own, may be downgraded or made surplus while the employers are enjoying such federal assistance.

5. Trade Adjustment Assistance (TAA) should be paid only to employees who are taking positive steps to obtain jobs in other industries (training, education, or relocation). However, the federal and state governments should counsel TAA-eligibles with regard to (a) the likelihood of exhausting benefits before being rehired, (b) the kinds of preparation needed in order to enter an occupation that is likely to remain in demand, and (c) local sources of education and training.

6. When employers submit a proposal for a major government contract, they should be required to make appropriate provision for the security of employees (other than those hired as temporaries) who are hired to perform the contract and who, at the expiration of the contract, are downgraded or made surplus through no fault of their own.

7. When employers claim accelerated depreciation of physical assets, they should be required to show that they have provided appropriately for the security of regular employees who, through no fault of their own, were downgraded or made surplus as a result of the introduction of those assets.

8. The rules of ERISA should be amended to provide that when employees are dismissed through no fault of their own, they do not lose their unvested pension rights. If an employer's

pension plan does not already make such provisions, employer and employee should be required to work out a mutually agreeable arrangement for the employee to retain such rights in the plan until retirement, or to transfer them into the next employer's pension plan, an IRA, or a similar deferred-compensation account.

9. All employers should be required to pay a reasonable amount of severance to employees who, without fault, either are dismissed or laid off for 12 months or more. Preferably, severance pay should be service-based, at the minimum level of one week for every year of service.

Recommendation 24: We recommend that employers and local and international unions jointly lobby for STC laws in those states that have not yet adopted them.

Recommendation 25: We recommend that employers and local and international unions jointly lobby Congress and the legislatures of STC states to make STC payable for a limited period to otherwise-eligible employees during unpaid hours (1) for voluntary on-the-job training, (2) for remedial education, (3) for skill development or continuing education, (4) for supplementing the partial wages of employees who perform work which is substantially less valuable than their normal work, and (5) when they are receiving outplacement assistance.

Recommendation 26: The federal government should assist employers who have given an explicit commitment of employment security against business declines. The assistance should consist of reimbursement for the net additional costs they incur as a result of retaining employees instead of laying them off or dismissing them during a recession. This federal subsidy of employment security will require time and financial limits. However, the gross costs will be offset by savings in income-transfer and retraining programs, and by the continuation of tax revenues from employed workers.

HOW TO MANAGE EMPLOYMENT SECURITY

TEMPORARY DECLINES

Actions in Response

Restricting hiring

Intensifying marketing efforts

Assigning employees lower-priority tasks

Training employees for flexible assignments

PERMANENT DECLINES

Actions in Response

Develop new products   Work sharing

Establish subsidiaries   Early retirement

Subcontract for other companies   Phased retirement

Restrict hiring   Productivity programs

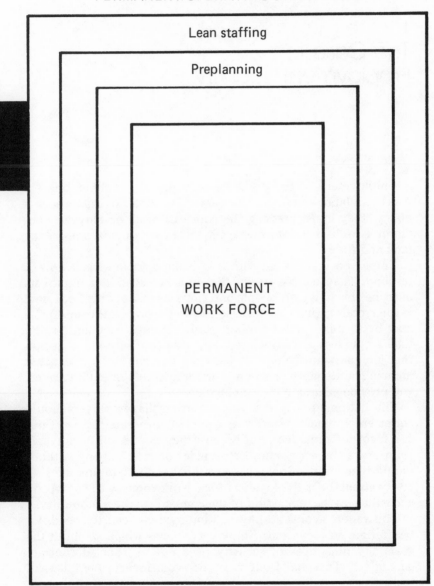

PERMANENT OPERATING STRATEGIES

Lean staffing

Preplanning

PERMANENT
WORK FORCE

1.
The Case for
Employment Security

Employment security has become priority number one for American labor unions at the bargaining table. In urging such a policy, they are expressing the concerns of all employees, non-union as well as union, managers and supervisors as well as the rank and file.

Employers confronted with this demand are uncertain how to respond. They believe firmly that in a free economy employers must be able to lay off people or dismiss them, not only because it is their prerogative but because the well-being of the enterprise may be at stake. On the other hand, although they understand that employees feel insecure, they have the erroneous notion that anyone who really tries hard can find another job and that income maintenance programs, such as unemployment insurance, will provide adequate interim income.

This national policy study report argues that employers should adopt employment security as a part of corporate strategy—not as a favor to employees, but because increasing security can serve to improve the economic performance of the company without diminishing its freedom. It argues further that employment security strengthens the loyalty of the work force to the company and enhances the reputation of the company in the community.

This report avoids absolutes. Employment security need not be lifetime employment. Employer policies which spell out the goals and objectives of security need not be ironclad contract guarantees. The goal itself must be evolutionary, flexible, and realistic.

In the world economy of the eighties, economic performance requires keeping up with the accelerated rate of change. Companies must frequently change their products, technology, processes of production, marketing, and dynamic relations with customers, suppliers, shareholders, and employees. Their survival depends on the ability to constantly adapt and readapt.

The ability to change with the times and with the state of the art depends, first and foremost, on the cooperation of the employees who operate the business day to day. Employees generally are not averse to change—as a matter of fact, they welcome it, provided that their jobs are secure. However, when change carries with it the threat of job loss, they will resist it, overtly or covertly.

As change is the key to corporate success, so employment security for all employees, including managers and executives, is the key to cooperation. With such a policy, employees feel free to participate enthusiastically in the change process and even to initiate change.

The incentive for employers to embark on this course of action should be the knowledge that companies that have managed to create secure environments are among the world's most prosperous and their employees, among the world's most productive.

The Example of New Lanark (1800-1825) and Beyond

The link between employment security, technological change, and productivity improvement was demonstrated by Robert Owen as early as the beginning of the nineteenth century. Owen, an Englishman, became a part owner and manager of a cotton mill in New Lanark, Scotland, in 1800, when the Scots regarded the English as the enemy. Conditions in the workplace and in the homes of the workers appalled him.

> Owen reported: "I thought there would be no termination to the changes required. I soon found that a reconstruction of the whole establishment would be necessary for my views, and for the pecuniary success of the concern. The evil conditions which I had to contend against were the ignorance, superstition, and consequent immoral conduct and bad habits of the great majority of the population; the long day's work which they had to undergo; the inferior qualities and high price of everything which they had to purchase for their own use; the bad arrangements in their houses for

rearing and training their children from their birth through infancy and childhood; and their prejudices against an English manufacturer becoming a hard task master, as they imagined I was going to be, because they saw I was going to adopt what they called new-fangled measures. The work people were systematically opposed to every change which I proposed, and did whatever they could to frustrate my object."

Owen slowly began to make progress, but the majority of the workers were still suspicious, feeling that his innovations were just a new way of trying to squeeze greater productivity out of them. A climactic event . . . brought a radical change in the workers' attitudes and an end to their suspicions. This was an American embargo on cotton in 1806. . . . The master spinners [the manufacturers] had to decide either to pay inordinately high prices for raw materials with the risk of a great drop in price when supplies resumed, or stop their machines and fire the workers. Most did the latter. Owen stopped the machinery but continued to pay full wages for keeping the machinery clean and in good working condition. He continued to do so until the embargo was ended, four months later. In this way, he won the full confidence of his workers and was able to go ahead much more rapidly with his innovations. . . .[1]

On the strength of this intuitive "no-layoff policy," Owen was able to introduce a wide range of managerial and organizational improvements, and one technical innovation after another, in rapid succession. The bottom line was that the New Lanark mill averaged a 20 percent annual return on investment from 1800 to 1825.[2]

In the United States, several dozen companies of varied sizes and in different industries have been known to follow Owen's no-layoff policy. Some have done so for decades, which argues that employment security is not only useful but feasible. The list of pacesetting companies shown here includes a surprising number of household names. Its completeness, of course, cannot be certified.

Caveats

Some companies have maintained an extensive no-layoff policy and later modified or abandoned it in the face of economic problems. Among them are Tektronix, Eastman Kodak, Procter &

The Pacesetters

ADVANCED MICRO
DEVICES

AVON PRODUCTS

BANK OF AMERICA

BELL LABORATORIES

CHAPPARAL STEEL

CONTROL DATA

DANA

DATA GENERAL

DELTA AIRLINES

DIGITAL EQUIPMENT
CORPORATION

DU PONT

EASTMAN KODAK

EXXON

FEDERAL EXPRESS

FEL PRO

GORDON RUPP

HALLMARK

HEWITT ASSOCIATES

HEWLETT-PACKARD

HOOD MILK

IBM

INTEL

S.C. JOHNSON

LEVI STRAUSS

ELI LILLY

LINCOLN ELECTRIC

MALLINCKRODT

MATERIALS RESEARCH
CORPORATION

HERMAN MILLER

MOTOROLA

NISSAN U.S.

NUCOR

LGA

PEOPLE EXPRESS

POLAROID

PROCTER & GAMBLE

QUILL

R.J. REYNOLDS
TOBACCO

TANDEM COMPUTERS

TEKTRONIX

TENNANT

3M

UPJOHN

WYETH LABORATORIES

Gamble, Polaroid, and the Dana Corporation. Their change of course is often cited as evidence that employment security is a risky business. Yet they are the first to testify to the achievements of these policies.

The General Motors/UAW agreement of 1982, in particular, has elicited warnings, according to the Bureau of National Affairs (BNA). The BNA has referred to the comments of two business leaders and an economist as evidence. For example, Alexander B. Trowbridge, president of the National Association of Manufacturers, it says, has described the guaranteed-jobs provision of the agreement as "very dangerous."

"Guaranteed jobs can mean enormous costs, reduced flexibility in management and investment decisions, and reduced funds available for technological modifications to increase productivity," said Trowbridge.

Edward L. Cushman, former American Motors vice-president for labor relations, agrees, says the BNA. "The hard cold fact in an economy changing so rapidly," Cushman points out, "(is that) job security is dependent on the employer's competitive ability and on economic forces beyond the employer's control."

MIT Professor Thomas Kochan is also quoted as saying that job guarantees would be particularly risky "on the downside," with the costs likely to get out of hand during a major recession.[3]

Those warnings must be taken seriously, indeed. But, at the same time, one must bear in mind that they apply to a particular type of employment security commitment, namely, a full guarantee against layoffs and dismissals, regardless of external economic conditions. The risks in a blanket guarantee are enormous, since every company is at the mercy of the federal government's stop-and-go economic policies and many are in highly cyclical industries.

The thrust of the present report is that a firm can stop well short of a blanket guarantee and still provide sufficient employment security to elicit employee commitment to continual change. A firm can provide employment security even when dismissals are unavoidable. Furthermore, it can achieve a good part of the objective by starting with a modest commitment and gradually extending it as the economic means become available. Our definition of employment security is much broader, more flexible, and permits tailor-made adaptations appropriate to each company's economic circumstance.

A Definition of Employment Security

Discussion of employment security is plagued by the unclear and conflicting uses of familiar phrases, such as continuous employment, full employment, guaranteed work, job security, and income security. It suffers also from the fact that speakers and writers use the term "employment security" as if it meant one particular technique, such as "lifetime" employment, civil service status, academic tenure, or the guaranteed annual wage.

In this report, employment security means a *continuum* rather than a single fixed point. The extent of employment security in a given organization should be measured by the degree to which employees have the *assurance that, regardless of internal or external changes, they will continue in employment* as long as they live up to the terms and conditions of employment. Very few employers provide absolutely no employment security; no employer provides absolute employment security.

Within our definition, an infinite number of variations may exist, depending on several factors:

☐ *Different classes of employees* may enjoy different degrees of employment security. For example, managers normally have greater security than blue-collar employees.

☐ *Permanent* employees have more employment security than temporary employees.

☐ *Length of service* may determine the degree of security. For example, at Lincoln Electric employees with less than two years of service are not entitled to the generally guaranteed number of annual working hours.

☐ Certain *changes*, but not others, may be covered. For example, employees may be secure against technological changes, but not against plant closures.

☐ *Occupation and wages may be altered.* Employees may be assured of permanent employment, but not necessarily in the current position or occupation or at the current wage level, and not necessarily with the current employer.

☐ *Employment may be offered in a different location.* For example, a displaced employee may be transferred to a different job in the same community by outplacement to a different employer.

☐ Certain *aspects of employment* may be protected and not others, such as weekly earnings, an hourly rate, a minimum number of working hours per year, and so on. Thus, the job is protected, but the terms of employment are modified temporarily.

☐ Security may be contingent on *acceptance of certain conditions,* such as mandatory overtime, internal transfer at management's discretion, and blurring of jurisdictional lines.

☐ *Negotiated concessions* may be required, such as wage reductions, benefit modifications, and work-rule relaxations.

☐ Security may apply for a *limited period of time* (such as, for the duration of a collective agreement), or for the work life of the employee (as in the case of the newspaper typographers, longshoremen, and others).

The term *job security* is avoided in this report because of its ambiguity. Sometimes people use the term in the same sense that we use employment security. Often, however, they also use it to mean that employees have a legal right to remain permanently in their current positions or occupations, which, in our view, is impractical for a modern free economy. It is also too narrow and rigid as compared with employment security.

We also distinguish employment security from *income security,* because the two concepts relate to different problems. Employment security is concerned with continuation of employment, while income security is concerned with continuation of income for people who have been downgraded, have lost their employment, or have been unable to find employment in the first instance.

Table 1, in the appendix, illustrates some of the better-known points along the continuum.

Scope of This Report

The focus of this report is microeconomic: namely, it emphasizes what employers, employees, and unions can do to ensure that people currently employed continue in employment, and what government can do to reinforce these programs. The report does not deal, except indirectly, with macroeconomic issues that bear on employment security but require separate study.

The critical national debate regarding full employment is linked directly to monetary and fiscal policy, and to the trade-off between inflation and unemployment. This is a macroeconomic issue of major proportion, with profound economic, political, and social consequences. Although a full-employment goal for the American economy has been established by national legislation, it has not been achieved, nor is it likely to be achieved in the near future. Another unresolved macroeconomic issue related to employment security is the desirability of a national industrial policy, the outcome of which will hinge to a large degree on the 1984 presidential election rather than on economic theories or judgments.

To attempt to address these issues within the framework of this policy study would only detract from its objective: finding the means to provide employment security through the actions of individual employers and unions.

Although the Institute is fully committed to a continuing analysis of the economy, and especially the conditions of employment and productivity of the American work force, it is not the purpose of this study to advocate changes of macroeconomic policy as the means to employment security. We believe that the greatest opportunity for constructive results lies within the thousands of employing organizations in America, if they will take the initiative and embrace employment security as a corporate strategy rather than as a social necessity. As a spur to such action, however, we do recommend major changes to bring federal treatment of employers and employees into more equitable balance with respect to taxation of capital losses, import protection, export subsidies, and other government interventions.

Pressure for Employment Security Will Continue

In organizations whose employees are represented by a union, joint employer-union planning and action on matters of employment security are in the interests of both parties. Pressure for it originates mainly from organized labor at the bargaining table. This reflects the response of negotiators to the felt need of the membership, who have raised employment security to the number-one issue on the list of bargaining demands. In fact, UAW President Owen Bieber, in his address to the UAW's special collective bargaining convention in March 1984, called increased job security a "top priority goal."[4]

Now that employment security is at the top of the unions' agenda, it must be addressed in a useful and effective manner. Massive layoffs, the ugly residue of the 1980-82 recession, have created a new urgency to provide stronger insurance for the individual against the vicissitudes of competition. The combined force of deregulation and tougher foreign competition is still keenly felt by workers. The impact on autos and steel and heavy manufacturing has radiated to firms that supply them materials and services and will inexorably penetrate other parts of the American economy.

Leading American corporations, such as IBM and Ford, are building their strategies for the future on the assumption that international competition will intensify, especially as more developing countries learn the secrets of competitive mass production.

Pressures for an improved form of employment security are nearing the boiling point. These issues are not only on the front burner in many negotiations but are also the hidden agenda for the overwhelming majority of employees who are not represented by unions. That workers and unions are in dead earnest about this issue is evident from the many recent agreements in which they have traded off wages, benefits, and work rules for employment security. The willingness to make painful economic sacrifices, unprecedented in our economic history over the past 40 years, has refuted the belief that wages and benefits are inflexible on the down side.

These experiences teach us—the hard way—that employees are willing to give a lot of themselves for the sake of career employment. Thus, employment security has the potential to elevate the level of employee commitment to the organization and to reinforce the mutual goals of the organization and the employee.

Major collective agreements signed in recent years attest to the high value employees set on employment security:

□ *International Brotherhood of Teamsters/National Master Freight agreement.* Work-rule revisions, suspensions of COLAs, and no pay raises for three years, in exchange for a promise not to establish nonunion subsidiaries and the extension of seniority protection for laid-off truckers.

□ *United Food & Commercial Workers/Armour, Wilson, Hormel.* Wages frozen and COLAs deferred, in exchange for a promise not to close any packing houses for the next 18 months and advance notice of closings thereafter.

□ *Printing unions/Standard Gravure.* Five-year moratorium on wage increases and suspension of restrictive practices, in exchange for a promise to invest in new equipment and start a profit-sharing plan.

☐ *Allied Industrial Workers/Dana (Fort Wayne axle plant).* Labor costs to be reduced by $2 million per year, to avoid shutdown.

☐ *United Rubber Workers/*
  Uniroyal. COLAs forgone and wages and benefits to be held below those of other major rubber companies, in exchange for comparable sacrifices by white-collar employees and executives.
  Goodyear. Wage, benefit, and work-rule concessions, in exchange for an agreement to build a plant in Akron and expand in Topeka.
  Indianapolis Rubber. Pay cuts and suspension of COLAs, in exchange for keeping the plant open.

☐ *United Steelworkers/*
  McLouth. Wage cuts, suspension of COLAs and some time off, in exchange for agreement by the company (in bankruptcy) to open its books.
  Timken. Eleven-year moratorium on strikes in the Canton plant, in exchange for a promise not to build a plant in the South.

☐ *United Auto Workers/*
  Federal Forge. Suspension of four paid holidays and COLAs, to avoid shutdown.
  American Motors. Wage and benefit increases deferred for three years, in exchange for a promise to keep its plants open for the duration of the contract, to handle all reductions in force (RIFs) through attrition (except those due to reduced sales), and to give 60-days' notice before outsourcing.
  General Motors. Wage increases and COLAs deferred, in exchange for a promise to reopen four plants, a guaranteed income stream for high-seniority workers, lifetime guaranteed employment experiments for 80 percent of the work force at four plants, intensive communication between the head of the UAW/GM department and the General Motors board of directors, transfer of laid-off workers, and profit sharing.
  Ford Motor Company. In an agreement that set the pattern for GM-UAW, three Ford plants were designated

for experiments in lifetime guaranteed employment for 80 percent of the work force. In the Rawsonville, Michigan, plant in March 1984, employees accepted an alternative solution: the entire work force is guaranteed at least 32 hours per week plus full benefits for three and one-half years, in exchange for flexible assignment rights, special training programs, consolidation of skilled trades into basic trades, and establishment of work teams.

☐ *Amalgamated Clothing & Textile Workers/Xerox.* Pay and COLAs frozen for one year and restrained for the next two years, less generous health insurance, work-rule changes, abandonment of some personal holidays, and absenteeism controls, in exchange for guaranteed employment for the duration of the contract.

☐ *Communications Workers of America/AT&T.* A strike led to agreement on a training program for displaced workers, career-development training for all workers, and income supplements for high-seniority displaced workers.

☐ *IBEW/Potomac Electric Power Company.* Flexible work rules, in exchange for a promise of no layoffs or pay cuts for unionized workers with twelve and one-half years' seniority.

It should be noted that "concessions" are accepted by the membership only when unions see them as the means of salvaging a desperate situation. If they believe that jobs are permanently going down the tube, they fight to maintain the status quo.

Pressure will come from white-collar employees, too. Over 16 percent of the work force are classified as professional/technical. Surveys reveal that this group is very concerned about business cycles and feels threatened by periodic campaigns to cut personnel costs. In fact, the 1980-82 recession adversely affected a greater proportion of white-collar, professional, and managerial personnel than ever before. This has also been reflected to some degree in increased unionization of professionals.[5]

Onus on Employers

In Europe, the reluctance of employers to provide employment security at plant level has led to restrictive legislation on layoffs, dismissals, and plant closings. In the United States, there have been numerous proposals for state and federal legislation on advance notice of plant closings. But American employers dislike legislative rigidities as much as American workers dislike

Japanese-style checks on their freedom to change employers. (One in five U.S. employees change their *occupations* every five years.[6])

Western European countries have tried to relieve employment insecurity through a combination of government interventions and nationally negotiated collective agreements. They have not so much ensured continued employment as made layoffs and dismissals cumbersome and expensive. It is useful for employers to give advance notice of reductions in force and to support a process of consultation and planning with representatives of the workers in order to arrive at just solutions. It is unfortunate, however, that the procedure has to be enforced by severe penalties and be subject to bureaucratic and judicial obstructions.

The solutions usually consist of various forms of income security: short-time compensation for reduced workweeks; substantial payments for "redundancy"; and early retirement for employees approaching normal retirement age. The European systems provide much more *income* security than the U.S. system, but there is no evidence that companies which provide only income security enjoy greater loyalty or commitment to change than their U.S. counterparts. Income security helps, but it is not equivalent to employment security.

In some instances, however, employers and unions have gone beyond the requirements and devised solutions in the nature of employment—rather than income—security. Several are mentioned in this report and developed more fully in the companion casebook, *Employment Security in Action: Strategies That Work* by Jocelyn F. Gutchess (New York: Pergamon Press, 1985). These examples will gain prominence as European economies strive to become more flexible and creative and to free business from government red tape.[7]

It is in the interest of the free-enterprise system to move forward and develop a flexible approach to employment security. While no single employer or small number of employers can change the system, many major employers acting together can. For example, the Fortune 1000 companies alone comprise over 23 million employees. The best way to keep federal regulation out of employment security is to preempt the field by setting an example of enlightened corporate action. Continued lobbying to withstand legislative reform is a negative response justified only in terms of the status quo "right to hire and fire" philosophy.

The Income Security System Is Inadequate

Today the U.S. economy is governed by a system of employment at will (even when it is regulated by collective agreement), combined with unemployment insurance, severance, early retirement, Social Security and, in a few companies, Supplementary Unemployment Benefits. This income security system does not, and cannot, elicit employee commitment to continual change. Few employees believe the system will protect them if their employers decide they have become surplus to company needs. Their opinion is well founded.

Some 70 million nonunion workers in the United States, managerial as well as nonmanagerial, are employees at risk: Their employers have the right to fire them at any time for any cause, or for economic reasons. Nothing so clearly epitomizes the situation as the fact that the U.S. Bureau of Labor Statistics classifies the guaranteed workweek as a form of employment security. The guaranteed workweek is a promise that an employee who works a stated number of hours in a given week is entitled to work (or to be paid for) the remainder of the workweek.

Layoffs and dismissals have been the standard solution, not only in recent recessions but for many years, for union and nonunion employees alike. In manufacturing, where layoffs most frequently occur, the reported rate of layoffs per 100 employees per year, over the period 1968-1981, fluctuated between 0.9 and 2.1; the mean duration ranged between 6.8 weeks and 14.5 weeks.[8]

Traditionally in U.S. companies, a double standard has existed with regard to employment security, as manifested by the terms "salaried" and "hourly." Salaried employees, as a reward for being "part of management," remain on the payroll, while hourly workers ebb and flow with the volume of business.

A good case can be made that managers, whose decisions have much more bearing on the success of a firm than any actions of the rank and file, should receive less rather than more employment security. Indeed, in American and Japanese companies with no-layoff policies, managers are considered to have failed if layoffs become necessary in their work units. However, *in*security is as counterproductive for managers as for blue-collar employees. Managers' performance should be monitored as rigorously as the performance of any other employees, but there must be clear criteria, formal reviews, and documentation. Otherwise, managers will avoid taking necessary risks, and their anxiety will transmit itself down the line.

Union members and employees with statutory protection (women, minorities, handicapped people) are not subject to arbitrary dismissal, but in most other respects they, too, are employees at risk. The employer can lay off or dismiss any employee who has become surplus as a result of labor-saving improvements, external circumstances, or any other change in the business. Although a union contract governs procedures for layoff or dismissal, it does not (in most cases) otherwise circumscribe the employer's freedom to reduce numbers at will. Only 15 percent of collective agreements provide advance notice of shutdown or the introduction of new technology, and most of these specify one week's notice.[9]

In recent years, courts have been increasingly willing to probe the written and spoken words of employers to see whether a dismissed employee was implicitly or explicitly promised something more permanent than employment at will. When they find such a promise, the employee is given an opportunity to prove the dismissal was unwarranted. Damages for unjust dismissal can be high. Consequently, many nonunion companies are introducing formal procedures for performance appraisal, and grievance procedures similar to those established by union contracts.[10]

The fact remains, however, that employers can lay off or dismiss any worker for any business reason, without regard to individual performance or years of service. It goes without saying that an employer can dismiss any employee who *is* at fault.

Employee objections to the income security system include the following:

1. *Replacement jobs.* One assumption behind the existing system is that any competent worker can always find another job. The reality is that, except during periods of abnormally low unemployment, laid-off or dismissed workers have great difficulty in securing satisfactory replacement jobs. And often, when a new job is found, it takes several years to work back up to the former wage level. They get little help from the federal-state employment services. Whether a worker's difficulty is due to lack of suitable openings in the area, lack of skill in job search, or lack of the occupational skills that are in demand, the result is often a lengthy

period of unemployment. Thus, the fear of potential layoff or dismissal weighs heavily on a work force at risk, most of all in cyclical industries and in companies enduring fierce competition. The psychological and economic penalties of unemployment are not offset by prospects for replacement jobs. The replacement option is only attractive to especially high-talent people, a tiny fraction of the work force.

2. *Replacement of earnings.* In most states, unemployment insurance compensation replaces less than half of previous net earnings, and none of the fringe benefits (which average 20 percent to 40 percent of earnings). Most dismissed employees lose their health-care coverage and face the terrifying prospect of a major illness with devastating financial costs. In addition, employees with low seniority lose their pension credits. The duration of unemployment compensation is 39 weeks, usually extended during general recessions. However, during 1983, with unemployment approaching 11 percent, only 45 percent of the unemployed were receiving benefits. Unemployment insurance benefits prevent severe hardship, but they are no substitute for employment.

3. *Loss of seniority.* For women and minorities, layoff has a compound effect. They are the last hired, so they are also the first fired. With low earnings and savings, they often cannot hold out long enough to be recalled; so they take the first job that comes along and start again at a lower wage, with zero seniority. Consequently, interrupted employment carries several penalties and, inversely, employment security carries many rewards.

4. *Older workers.* Employees aged 40 and over face even greater difficulty in finding a suitable new job. Those old enough to qualify for early Social Security or disability will often grasp such benefits as the only way out. The dramatic decline in the participation rate of men aged 55 to 64 reflects the adverse effects of job loss on lifetime opportunity for older men. With only a 69.4 percent participation rate, more than one-fourth of all men in this age group are out of the labor force (see p. 110).

5. *Loss of respect.* Even if the other inadequacies could be remedied, there is no way to make up for the loss of self-respect that Americans experience when they lose a job. A job is the source of social status as well as income.

6. *Economic consequences.* The income security system affects employers, too, because aside from being unable to induce employee commitment to continual change, it is expensive and

inflationary. Employers tend not to realize how expensive, because many of the costs show up as taxes rather than costs of production. When employees are laid off or dismissed, not only their earnings but their emotional and physical lives deteriorate, and the repair bills fall on local, state, and federal government.

Increased layoffs and dismissals directly affect employers through their payment of unemployment insurance taxes. They are somewhat aware of other direct costs, such as bumping, severance, retirement, and so on. They are less aware that every one percent increase of unemployment costs the federal government budget $37 billion net, including the loss of revenues. No single employer can cause a one percent rise in unemployment, but employers collectively do. State and local governments also feel the pinch.

7. *Physical and mental consequences.* That employees' physical and mental health suffers during unemployment has been well documented. For example, K.H. Blair, after close study of large-scale layoffs in the Seattle area, wrote:

> Few life experiences are so profoundly damaging as long-term joblessness. Symptoms of unemployment stress include depression, mental illness, family conflict and violence, crime, drug and alcohol abuse, and certain health disorders. These by-products propel some of the jobless and their family members into the social-service, health-care, and criminal-justice systems. Job-seeking efforts may be ineffective when suicidal preoccupation, interpersonal family conflict, high blood pressure, heart disease, and substance abuse become overriding problems. Eventually, some unemployed persons simply change their label as a jobless person for that of patient, parolee, or social-service client.
>
> Workers who have been laid off may present special problems to the employer who hopes to recall them and the community which must support them. While some employers often feel absolved of responsibility . . . because of their payment of the unemployment insurance tax, the magnitude of such contributions is dwarfed by the cost of joblessness to the community in such social-welfare expenditures as welfare, food stamps, and Medicaid, as well as in lost tax revenue. . . . The personal impact of joblessness may become disabling for some workers so that when they are recalled

they may return with stress-induced health problems, drug or alcohol addiction, marital strife, mental-health problems, and bankruptcy."[11]

The U.S. Senate has received statistical evidence from Dr. Harvey Brenner of Johns Hopkins University, who "has studied the effects of long-term unemployment on the health of the population. He found that when unemployment rose one percentage point, suicides increased 4.1 percent; homicides 5.7 percent; death from heart disease, liver cirrhosis, and other stress-related disorders, 1.9 percent; and 4.3 percent more men and 2.3 percent more women were admitted to mental hospitals. These alarming figures, compiled from an analysis of 30 years of data, suggest a wide array of serious problems that may manifest themselves long after a recession ends.[12]

Local and state governments and community-based organizations are left to cope with the suffering. All of these programs cost money, which means higher taxes and charitable contributions. As individual and corporate taxpayers, employers pick up a large part of the tab. The money goes to support people who *want* to work but are effectively barred from creating goods and services: a formula for inflation and social disorder.

It would be unrealistic to look for significant improvements in the existing security system in the foreseeable future:

☐ The U.S. Employment Service would require a huge infusion of money and management resources for many years before it could function as a true placement agency. It would also need the cooperation of employers, who now refuse to divulge information about present and future vacancies.

☐ To increase the amount or duration of unemployment insurance benefits would raise taxes substantially. The federal budget deficit clouds any prospects for such an increase for many years to come.

While the income security system can be modified to facilitate employer efforts to expand employment security, as described in chapter 8, the real need is corporate commitment to expand employment security. The basic rationale for employer policy is economic self-interest, not social service.

Employment Security: Key to Continual Change

In the long run, enlightened employers will choose employment security because it induces employees to support continual change and it creates and sustains a more competitive company. Although the leading Japanese companies are most often cited in support of this assertion, one need look no farther than some of the great American companies from which the Japanese learned: IBM, Lincoln Electric, Exxon, DuPont, Eastman Kodak, and 3M. IBM, in particular, has passed through several radical changes of product lines and processes, grown enormously, and become truly international; thousands of its people have transferred from one function to another as well as from one location to another, all with conspicuous success and high morale. The company's typewriter division has stayed ahead of the competition by maintaining quality while continually reducing production costs.

IBM illustrates that employment security is *compatible* with rapid productivity improvement through labor-saving changes. On a much smaller scale, Lincoln Electric has sustained a rapid increase of productivity in the manufacture of arc-welding equipment for almost 50 years, with no layoffs or dismissals. Both companies claim that employment security *facilitates* productivity improvement. Neither they nor we, however, claim that employment security *causes* productivity improvement, or any other kind of performance improvement. Performance improvement stems from managerial skills, judgment, leadership, and hard work. Employee cooperation converts management leadership into action. The great value of employment security is that it stimulates employees to cooperate for the success of the firm and eliminates the nagging fear of job loss. A poorly managed company that undertakes employment security will simply continue to be poorly managed.

Employment security encourages the cooperation of employees by freeing them to:

☐ Accept management-proposed changes that might otherwise threaten security.

☐ Volunteer ideas for improving performance and productivity, even when labor-saving changes may result, and may, in fact, initiate labor-saving changes.

☐ Maintain an optimal pace of work, without fear that the job may run out.

☐ Give up restrictive practices (such as jurisdictional lines and obsolete work rules), which are designed to protect jobs.

☐ Agree to perform tasks outside their normal job definition, when there is need to do so.

☐ Accept inconveniences, such as mandatory overtime, when persuaded of the need.

☐ Volunteer for, and profit from, training that expands the boundaries of their jobs.

Employers benefit from employment security in other practical ways:

☐ The increased flexibility of employment made possible by employment security can enrich the job, thereby improving both QWL and productivity. Good examples are craft consolidation among maintenance workers (for example, electricians agree to perform related carpentry and millwright tasks), and semi-autonomous work teams for operators, in which task assignments become interchangeable. In addition, broadening the job strengthens the employee's occupational skills and potential in the labor market, which adds to long-term employment security.

☐ The organization benefits because today's competitive market demands continual investment in training and retraining, and employment security helps it to view employees as permanent and, therefore, as a capital investment in a real asset. (Corporate accounts show physical resources as assets and liabilities; employees are shown only as costs.) Secure employees are less likely to walk away, carrying the employer's investment with them. Moreover, well-trained employees become the trainers of new employees. The continuity of skill, experience, and group relations over the years creates a unique pool of talent and commitment which, in turn, results in a major competitive advantage.

☐ Managers, supervisors, and employees gain a new perspective and a higher level of trust in each other, as employment security helps them concentrate on the common goal: the success of the enterprise.

☐ Employment security enhances the employer's image by contributing to the stability of the community. Ready recourse to layoffs has the opposite effect.

☐ Employment security puts the employer in a position to move rapidly when a business downturn ends. Some of the inroads made by Japanese companies into U.S. markets, such as electronics and integrated circuits, have come about because the Japanese had products for sale at the end of a recession which U.S. buyers wanted. Japanese companies benefited because U.S. companies had not yet returned to effective production.

☐ Employment security reduces the cost of employee turn-over. No-layoff companies have very low rates of turnover and do not lose their investment in employees. The costs of turnover, like those of layoffs and dismissals, are hidden in the costs of production and personnel management. They are reflected indirectly in waste of tools, equipment, energy, raw materials, and facilities.

All those involved gain advantages from avoiding layoffs:[13]

Advantages to Employers

1. Maintenance of productivity because of higher morale and preservation of employee skills.

2. Retention of skilled workers.

3. Reduction or elimination of the large costs associated with layoffs, particularly where "bumping" occurs; for example, distorted production scheduling, delayed start-ups when recession ends, retraining of bumped employees.

4. Greater flexibility in deploying human resources to keep operations going.

5. Savings in employer costs associated with severance pay, early-retirement incentives, and other layoff schemes requiring substantial financing.

6. Avoidance of post-recession costs of hiring and training new workers to replace those who found other jobs during layoff.

7. Reinforcing group loyalties and strengthening employee loyalty to the firm.

Advantages to Workers

1. Continued job attachment for workers who would otherwise have been laid off.

2. Continued fringe-benefit protection for employees and their families.

3. Retention of more minority and women workers, thus preserving the aims and achievements of affirmative action.

4. Security for older workers, who cost more, are often among the first fired in selective layoffs, and are discriminated against when they seek new jobs.

5. More effective preservation of the family income of two-paycheck families than if one member continues to work full time and the other is on unemployment insurance, particularly if the wife is a new entry into the labor force. (Women's traditional jobs are generally low paying, and eligibility rules for un-

employment insurance require workers to meet a combination of dollar amount and time in covered occupations. For some new entrants, these benefits may be low or nonexistent.)

Advantages to Unions

1. Greater bargaining flexibility when an employer suffers a downturn.

2. Greater ability to take into account diverse interests of membership and fairly represent all employees in the bargaining unit.

3. Improved long-run prospects for the union. Layoffs generally pose problems for unions because some laid-off workers do not return, new employees have to be organized, and returning workers may have less enthusiasm for the union after extended unemployment.

4. Less polarization between groups represented by the union.

5. Increased support from new workers who would otherwise be laid off.

6. Preservation of union membership and members' ability and willingness to pay dues.

Advantages to Society

1. Protection of affirmative action and equal employment opportunity advances.

2. Less need for public-service jobs.

3. Less need for public assistance for the unemployed.

4. No increase in the net costs of unemployment insurance.

5. Less disruption of the society as a whole.

6. A population healthier in mind and body.

A Mutually Advantageous Bargain

Lest there be any doubt, this report advocates employment security only for employees who have met the terms and conditions of employment.

We regard employment security as a mutually advantageous bargain between the employer and employees and unions, not as an entitlement. It works as long as the business prospers; and the business prospers only if employees at all levels pull their weight. Employees who perform poorly, behave insubordinately or incompetently, or in other ways fail in their duties cannot be said to pull their weight. They should therefore be excluded from protection—before the probationary period ends, if possible. On the other hand, no protected employee should be deprived of employment security without due process, in which the employer bears the burden of proof.

The future belongs to those who prepare for it. Employers who can build a secure and successful environment for their own work force can grow, achieve, and master the competitive world economy. Employers who accept insecurity and perpetuate a cyclical hire-fire approach to employment place their most valued assets at constant risk and pay the penalty in lost opportunity. The permanent investment that a career employee makes in the company merits a permanent commitment by the employer.

This policy study offers a strategy for achieving a realistic degree of employment security without penalty to the employer and with immense potential rewards for employees, shareholders, managers, and the community. An employment security policy requires commitment and steady nerves, but it is as valuable to the enterprise as long-term corporate investment strategy.

NOTES

1. E. Bruce Peters, "Job Security, Technical Innovation, and Productivity," *Personnel Journal* 57 (January 1978): 33-34.

2. Ibid.

3. Bureau of National Affairs, *Labor Relations in an Economic Recession: Job Losses and Concession Bargaining.* Special Report (Washington, D.C.: Bureau of National Affairs, 1982), p. 13.

4. "Job Security, Restoration Are Top Bargaining Goals for Auto Workers," *Daily Labor Report*, March 7, 1984, p. A8.

5. "Union Membership Grows among Professional, Technical Employees Working for Organizations," *Daily Labor Report*, March 9, 1984, p. A9.

6. Remarks by Ronald Kutscher, associate commissioner, Bureau of Labor Statistics, U.S. Department of Labor, at a meeting of The Productivity Forum (Work in America Institute) at Williamsburg, Virginia, March 27-29, 1984.

7. Paul Lewis, "Signs of European Economic Rebound Grow," *New York Times*, April 24, 1984, p. 1.

8. R.W. Bednarzik, "Layoffs and Permanent Job Losses: Workers' Traits and Cyclical Patterns," *Monthly Labor Review*

106 (September 1983): 3-12.

9. "Saving Plants and Jobs," *World of Work Report*, June 1984, p. 4.

10. Joann S. Lublin, "Firing Line: Legal Challenges Force Firms to Review Ways They Dismiss Workers," *Wall Street Journal*, September 13, 1983, p. 1.

11. "Layoffs and Social Work Intervention," *Urban & Social Change Review* 16 (Summer 1983): 9+.

12. D.W. Riegle, Jr., "The Psychological and Social Effects of Unemployment," *American Psychologist* 37 (October 1982): 1114.

13. Jerome M. Rosow and Robert Zager, *New Work Schedules for a Changing Society* (New York: Work in America Institute, 1981), pp. 89-90.

2.
The Commitment to
Employment Security

Although employers retain the prerogative to hire and fire, and—in the absence of a collective agreement—to hire and fire at will, they do not exercise these rights indiscriminately. Many employees stay with a single employer for years on end.

In 1978 almost 40 percent of all workers in the United States had been working *for their current employers* five years or longer; over 23 percent, ten years or longer. The figures are more than 5 percent higher when the job tenure of men alone is measured (the difference being accounted for by the great influx of women into the work force in the 1970s). The percentages for workers in manufacturing are higher still.[1]

Employers understand the costs of turnover: they know that the retention of qualified, productive employees is critical to corporate performance and that even the threat of downgrading or dismissal exerts a powerful drag on their employees' productivity.

Still, they have a deep conviction that giving up the prerogative of dismissal at will could mortgage their economic future. In their view, if undesirable employees (however defined) cannot be separated from the work force, their contagion will spread and infect all employees. They also fear that, no matter how much they might want to provide security, they cannot afford to have their hands tied if the firm's survival should be at stake.

So there is an impasse. Employees need assurance that their conditions of employment will not be impaired through no fault of their own. At the same time, employers need to be assured that withholding their trump card will not mean loss of control. In the present state of practice in America the employer is essentially able to respond to economic necessity, but employees are virtually unprotected and fall easy prey to business reverses and especially to economic recessions. They are even more vulnerable to dismissal at will by virtue of the trend toward specialization of the work force. At the same time, the nation lacks a specific response to the problem—either national policies or employment practices which suggest that we can manage our human resources more effectively.

The way out of the impasse is clear. The key is held by private corporations which, in the absence of national policy, should make a commitment to employment security that:

☐ Is explicit.

☐ Is accepted by employees as reliable, reasonable, and fair.

☐ Is realistically within the employer's ability to fulfill.

☐ Relieves employees' anxieties about working themselves out of a job.

☐ Allows the employer to downgrade or dismiss, without cumbersome procedures, those employees whose behavior deserves such treatment.

☐ Permits the employer flexibility to modify the commitment under unusual conditions of economic necessity.

AN EXPLICIT COMMITMENT

Whatever the particulars of the security an employer decides to provide, employers will gain more by spelling out their intentions in writing than by letting employees guess them. Security has as much to do with *knowing* where one stands as with the safety of the place where one is actually standing. As Professor R.H. Hayes has written:

> In most large U.S. companies, 30% to 40% of the work force has life-time employment, in the sense that any production worker who has worked for more than 10 years is almost never laid off. Rather than making that fact explicit, however, and using it to increase workers' sense of self-worth and their commitment to the company, we continue to refer to them as "hourly workers." We thereby imply they are expendable—which they aren't.[2]

The fact that an unstated policy has been adhered to in the past gives no assurance that it will be continued beyond today. Only by making a declaration can employers persuade employees that they intend to stick to the policy. Where employees are represented by a union, the contract is a logical place for the commitment.

Employers associate the idea of employment security with the idea of being unable to get rid of undesirable employees, because they think of tenured employment in public service as the epitome of security and they have heard how difficult it is to fire a public servant. Layoffs and reductions in force have become quite common, however, in the public sector. Employers also overlook the fact that, even in the private sector, union agreements contain detailed procedures on discipline, suspension, and firing. In spite of these, however, employers with a good reason for disciplining employees generally get their way. An explicit commitment clearly does not impede justified separations from the payroll.

Nor do employers have to fear that an explicit commitment might tie their hands and cause self-destruction in case of an organization-threatening emergency. A commitment need not promise complete and unconditional lifetime security; even those Japanese employers who offer lifetime security stop well short of that. It can specify the types of situations in which employers would feel justified in excusing themselves from compliance. It might, in fact, outline a mutually agreeable procedure for invoking a loophole clause—a legitimate exception to the rule. For example:

☐ Lincoln Electric Company's extensive guarantee "is practically devoid of loopholes. There is no escape except in the event of an unforeseeable act of God (for example, destruction of the plant by an unpreventable fire). Acts of God, per se, do not excuse." However, the company "can terminate or amend the guarantee . . . after six months' notice to employees and at the end of a calendar year."[3]

☐ IBM tells its employees that although it cannot *guarantee* continuation of its long-term policy of full employment (that is, employment security) to all of its employees, it "will leave no stone unturned in attempting to continue" that policy.[4]

☐ Another large company's handbook states: "There are wide seasonal variations in the demand for many company products.

In order to avoid, as far as possible, the effects of these variations upon stability of employment, the company gives continual attention to planning its production schedules. The result has been a marked stability of employment. Such planning cannot, of course, prevent reduced employment when business conditions are generally unfavorable or when the demand for company products is greatly reduced."[5]

☐ The chairman of Control Data Corporation stated, in a public speech: "Control Data will pursue a policy which provides an increasing level of job security to the greatest number of its

TEN REASONS FOR AN EMPLOYMENT SECURITY COMMITMENT

☐ Induces employees to support continual change and thereby makes for a more competitive company.

☐ Encourages employers to invest in training and developing people.

☐ Helps managers, supervisors, and workers to concentrate on the common goal: success of the enterprise.

☐ Enhances the employer's image in the community.

☐ Enables the employer to move rapidly when a business slump ends.

☐ Reduces the cost of turnover.

☐ Preserves skills and maintains productivity.

☐ Avoids the costs of "bumping" and related turmoil.

☐ Avoids the costs of income security.

☐ Avoids the costs of replacing people who leave in a layoff.

employees. . . . Immediate layoffs in response to a decline in business are becoming increasingly unacceptable in our society. . . . Nor is it acceptable to abruptly close plants as soon as there is a lack of need without reviewing reasons and possible alternatives with the affected community."[6]

☐ Advanced Micro Devices has promised that no one who has been with the company more than one year will be laid off for economic reasons.[7]

☐ The chairman of Materials Research Corporation gave a public pledge never to lay off any employee.[8]

Another potent reason for making the commitment explicit is that it wonderfully concentrates the mind of management. Living up to a policy of employment security—explicit or otherwise—is no easy task. It requires managers to plan the hiring, use, and release of employees with as much care as they give to money and physical resources (see chapter 3).

Anyone who has watched managers at work knows how painful they find the business of planning, not so much because it demands intellectual effort as because it is experienced as an interruption or frustration of action. Their resistance is strengthened because dealing objectively with people is more stressful than dealing with inanimate resources.

In addition, most managers have grown up in the tradition of assuming that hiring and firing are the day-to-day stuff of running a business, rather than actions to be taken only after long and careful thought. Even though they have an antipathy toward the distasteful task of dismissing employees, they accept it as their personal and professional responsibility.

For all these reasons, managers need encouragement and help in planning for employment security. An explicit corporate commitment supplies this support and creates a positive change in managerial goals.

HOW BROAD A COMMITMENT DO EMPLOYEES WANT?

Since employment security is a continuum rather than a fixed point, and since it is unrealistic to promise blanket protection, how broad must a commitment be in order for it to be worthwhile for employer and employees alike? The behavior of employees and unions furnishes clues to the answer.

Security against Productivity Improvements

As far back as records go, one of the principal bars to productivity improvement has been employees' fear of working themselves out of a job. They can understand why a firm might have to cut back the work force when business declines, but not why workers should lose income or jobs as a result of helping the employer make more money.

Many employers, when introducing productivity improvements, follow an undeclared policy of reducing the work force by attrition only. Others announce that policy but only on a case-by-case basis. Both of these courses leave employees uncertain and uneasy during the interim periods and surely deter them from volunteering ideas for labor-saving methods.

When employees talk about working themselves out of a job, they mean that if the firm becomes able to produce the same amount of output with fewer hours of labor, it will need fewer employees and will, therefore, lay some off. Underlying this fear are certain premises about the market for the firm's product or service:

☐ The market is fixed in size. For example, when our current construction contract is completed, the firm may not obtain another for some time.

☐ The market is highly competitive. Therefore, our market share of critical products may be reduced.

☐ The market may be elastic, but not elastic enough to offset our improved productivity, even if management reduces prices by the amount that higher productivity makes possible.

Given these premises and the absence of an explicit commitment, employees will, consciously or unconsciously, hold back some part of their potential contribution to the firm. Simple economic survival dictates that one does not act contrary to one's own interests. For example, employees who see a way of making their jobs (or other employees' jobs) unnecessary—whether through greater effort, a technical shortcut, or a whole new procedure—will first stop and ask themselves: What will happen to me as a result? Even if the company has usually protected its employees, how do I know that it will do so in my case? How do I know that my boss, or my boss's boss, hasn't been looking for a safe opportunity to fire me or shunt me into a less desirable job?

The same anxiety arises from other causes, too:

☐ If we improve quality and reduce the percentage of rejected parts, we won't have to make as many parts. Then we won't need as many workers making those parts.

☐ It will take a few months to get the bugs out of the new office machine, but once it's in full swing, half of my job will disappear. What then?

☐ My supervisor wants me to train that young woman who just joined the department. She's better educated than I am, and her salary is lower. Is it possible that they mean to have her replace me as soon as she's trained?

An employer may try to talk employees out of such fears by arguing that the market is larger and/or more elastic than they think. To which they may legitimately reply: "If you believe what you say, why don't you guarantee that you won't lay us off as a result of productivity improvement?"

And, in fact, when a firm makes such a promise, employees do cooperate much more wholeheartedly in reducing the labor content per unit of output.

☐ After the Buick Division in Flint, Michigan, guaranteed that employment security would not be harmed by productivity improvements, workers actively participated in designing and installing a new warehousing system, even though it was clear from the beginning that 20 of them would become surplus as a result.[9]

Within a year, over 120 Buick employees had volunteered for a minimum of 12 months' retraining in courses ranging from computers to basic education. Since entry into the Employee Development Center is regarded as an opportunity rather than a detour, people volunteer for assignment, and seniority applies.[10]

☐ In Italy, an agreement between the Fiat auto company and its unions, providing two years' paid retraining "leave" for employees displaced by technological or other changes, enabled the firm to raise performance enough to compete in the international market.[11]

☐ Over a period of 10 years, IBM's typewriter division reduced the number of employee hours per typewriter by 65 percent, reduced costs by 45 percent, and reduced warranty service calls by 50 percent. IBM today is the only major U.S. company manufacturing typewriters in this country.[12]

☐ At Lincoln Electric, where security is guaranteed and labor-saving changes are rewarded, it is not uncommon for employees to recommend the elimination of all or part of their own jobs.[13]

☐ At General Electric's aircraft engine plant in Lynn, Massachusetts, unionized draftsmen, designers, and planners—having been assured that labor surpluses would be handled through "attrition"—enthusiastically helped management to introduce advanced computer-aided-design equipment.[14]

☐ The quality-of-work-life programs at General Motors and Ford Motor Company continued to generate labor-saving improvements all through the 1980-82 recession because one of the promises made to UAW employees was that none would lose their jobs because of such improvements.[15]

☐ Nucor, a steel industry firm in the United States with productivity that rivals or exceeds its counterparts in Japan, has stayed at the technological forefront with the aid of a no-layoff policy. Employees work overtime to meet surges of demand, and occasionally work four-day or three-day weeks during a slump.[16]

The significance of this general rule is blurred by union attitudes when change is sought through new technology. Many collective bargaining agreements state that the union will not oppose management's introduction of potentially labor-saving or quality-improving technology and, according to a National Science Foundation study, unions live up to the agreements. However, the attitude expressed is nothing more than nonopposition, and nonopposition translates to nonparticipation. It means no more than it says, that is, employees will not stand in management's way—but neither will they do *more* than the minimum possible to help get the new technology into full operation quickly and smoothly.

The difference between neutrality and wholehearted cooperation can make a vast difference in productivity. If employers give their word that no layoffs or sharp pay reductions will result from the new technology, the road to active cooperation is wide open, particularly since employees can then view their role as a matter of self-interest: cooperating with the introduction of technology contributes to the competitiveness of the firm, which means, in turn, more security of employment for the individual and the union.

Security against Business Declines

Employee attitudes differ when jobs are threatened by a general falloff in the employer's business rather than by new technology. Their attitudes depend on (1) whether employees believe the employer's forecasts, (2) whether they consider the employer at fault for the decline of business (for example, failure to modernize equipment or to stay abreast of product/market changes versus a general economic recession), and (3) how long and deep they perceive their loss to be (for example, where income security is very strong, employees may feel little or no concern about a temporary decline). Attitudes will also be colored by whether employees believe the eventual cuts in labor hours will be a product of their past cooperation in improving productivity. Thus, instead of rewards, productivity would translate into punishment.

Much as American employees would like the comfort of knowing their employment will never be in jeopardy, they realize that such a guarantee is not always possible. When the survival of the firm is at stake for reasons beyond the employer's control, employees consider that the best one can ask for is an orderly, equitable procedure for allocating hardships, and as much help from the employer as possible in obtaining a suitable new job.

The difference between employee attitudes toward productivity-related threats and their attitudes toward market-related threats is clearly delineated by the comments of the local union president at Buick/Flint:

> Now we know that when we make changes in the workplace or when new technology comes in, those members affected will have the opportunity to upgrade themselves in the Employee Development Center [EDC] and then go on to innovative new job assignments. As we do this, there should be an understanding that fluctuation of the market does not put people into the EDC. If the market goes down, and that brings layoffs, the members would follow the regular flow chart, which we have always done. This is less likely to happen now because we are more competitive.[17]

HOW BROAD A COMMITMENT CAN AN EMPLOYER AFFORD?

The primary aim of an employer in giving a commitment to employment security is to win the sustained cooperation of employees. To have that effect, the commitment must be not only *credible* to employees but within the employer's capacity to deliver. Before committing themselves, therefore, employers should determine realistically how broad a commitment they can afford without losing credibility.

What the employer can afford, of course, is subject to change. A modest commitment given today may lead to performance improvements that enable the employer to give broader commitments later. Unforeseen business reverses may have the opposite effect.

In trying to gauge the costs of a commitment, the employer should follow the clue offered by employee attitudes: estimate separately the costs of commitments covering (1) productivity/performance improvements, (2) short-term business declines, and (3) long-term or permanent business declines.

Productivity/Performance Improvements

The cost of protecting employees against downgrading, layoff, and dismissals resulting from productivity/performance improvements tends to be grossly exaggerated. On a year-to-year basis, such improvements rarely exceed 6 percent per annum, unless business volume is growing even faster (in which case the firm faces a shortage rather than a surplus of labor).

Occasionally one comes upon horror stories about large numbers of jobs being eliminated or downgraded because of productivity/performance changes. As a rule, these occur in stagnant or declining industries, where the previous record of productivity growth has been especially bad and needed changes have been bottled up for years. When the dam finally breaks, all the accumulated waste of human resources must be dealt with at once, as in the case of longshoremen, typographers, and others swept up in "productivity bargains." What appears to be an overnight 50 percent gain in productivity is actually an accumulation of many years of normal productivity growth compressed into a year or two.

Another oversimplification is to attribute to the firm as a whole a productivity rise that affects only one part of the firm. A 50 percent productivity rise in one department may translate into a 5 percent rise for the firm. Since employees work for a firm, and not merely for a product line or a department, the consequent labor surplus is more manageable.

Any labor surplus caused by 6 percent per annum productivity increases can be offset by attrition (that is, not hiring people to replace employees who quit, retire, die, or leave for any reason other than layoff), even in a worst-case scenario. Nationally, quits average about 20 percent per annum, and other nonlayoff separations, about 6 percent per annum, with variations by industry and firm. The "quits" figure indicates the number of people who leave rather than the number of *positions* which are voluntarily vacated. A single position may have been occupied, in the course of a year, by several individuals in turn, each of whom has quit. But even if we cut the annual "quit" figure by half to account for this factor, more than enough people leave voluntarily to make it unnecessary to dismiss those who become surplus because of productivity improvements. Those who remain on the payroll may not have the skills to replace those who leave, but they can usually acquire them with adequate lead time for on-the-job training. The more restrictions on replacements by outside hiring, the greater the flexibility for retraining and redeploying existing personnel.

Managers may object that laying people off is a quick fix, whereas attrition/turnover works slowly. This is another illusion. As illustrated below, even if employees are fired without notice, their costs linger on for months, through unemployment insurance and other transfer payments.

In view of the clear net-cost advantage to employees and employer, we strongly recommend that employers guarantee that no permanent employee will be laid off or downgraded due to any labor surplus arising from internal corporate productivity/performance changes.

The performance enhancements made possible by such a commitment will help pay for increased security against business declines and will strengthen employee commitment to increase the company's competitive edge and market share.

Business Declines—Short-Term and Long-Term

Commitments to security despite business declines are inevitably riskier and more open-ended. The employer can estimate on the basis of past experience how long and deep a decline will be, but past experience is not always the most reliable guide. Still, some of the principal costs can be calculated with a high degree of accuracy.

In deciding what to do about employees who become surplus as a result of a business decline, the employer has no easy choices. Every decision represents a trade-off, in which one inevitable consideration is the baseline cost of laying people off temporarily or dismissing them permanently. For each location, employers should make, and keep up to date, calculations of the costs of layoff and dismissal. These costs will vary from state to state, and from one location to another, but the method of figuring them can be uniform and useful.

In strict bookkeeping terms, removing employees involuntarily from the payroll is far from cost-free, whether the removal is temporary (layoff) or permanent (dismissal). "Temporary" means that the employer expects sooner or later to recall the employees to work. An analysis based on the experiences of two major manufacturing corporations concluded that the hard cost of removing 100 shop-floor employees would amount to $741,500, or an average of $7,415 per employee removed.[18]

The costs were as follows:

State unemployment insurance	$600,000
Severance	49,000
Bumping	87,500
Administrative	5,000
	$741,500

In this table, "unemployment insurance" represents the increase in the employer's state tax liability because of the increase of 100 employees above the employer's normal rate of removal. "Severance" refers to the termination allowances provided by contract, based on length of service. "Bumping" costs reflect the loss of efficiency and quality, the essential retraining, and the protection of earnings of downgraded employees incurred as longer-service people step into positions vacated by shorter-service people until, finally, those with the shortest service go out. "Administrative" means additional costs due to the overtime and special efforts incurred in managing the program of layoff and dismissal.

The figures are understated insofar as they do not include the costs of recalling or replacing employees when a layoff ends. They omit, for example, the costs associated with *reverse* bumping (as the bumped employees find their way back to their pre-layoff slots) and the costs of recruiting, orienting, and training replacements for those who do not answer the recall notice.

When layoffs are proposed, line managers often fail to appreciate the size of the increase in state unemployment insurance. The company pays, in one form or another, *all* the unemployment insurance benefits collected by its employees, *plus* part of the state's administrative costs. And, because the tax imposed on companies increases in steps rather than evenly, a company's cost increase may significantly exceed the actual increase of benefits collected by its employees.

Against the costs of layoff and dismissal must be set the costs of alternative solutions available to the employer. The range of alternatives is wide—usually wider than assumed—and an employer can select any combination that makes the most sense in the circumstances. Costing each alternative is feasible. Indeed, some firms have established procedures for doing so.

GTE's EDCAM (Employment Dynamics Cost Analysis Model), for example, identifies numerous alternatives for dealing with the shortages and surpluses of a local work force and provides a formula to calculate the tangible and intangible costs of each alternative. Cost data can be maintained and updated as required. Alternatives are categorized according to whether they are suitable for short-term (up to six months) or long-term conditions.

Ten short-term options for surpluses are: restricting new hires, reducing overtime or part-time work, temporary assignments, temporary shutdown or layoff, excused absences, work sharing, transferring work in-house, reducing the workweek, retraining, and building inventory. Eight long-term options are: freezing hires, personnel transfers, voluntary-separation incentive programs, transferring work in-house, layoffs, outplacements, retraining, and job sharing.

The system helps the local manager identify cost factors, such as administrative costs of hiring, recall, transfer, layoff, and early retirement; costs of training; costs of inventory buildup; costs of "bumping" associated with layoffs; and many more. These factors, combined in various ways, make up the formulas for the total tangible costs of particular options. Other tangible but hard-to-quantify costs include: a decline in maintenance (especially preventive); increased scrap, repairs, and customer returns for poor quality; lost time and back-pay claims resulting from bumping grievances; and increased health-care costs, because employees have time to use their benefits and are afraid of losing them.

For example, the cost of a personnel transfer is calculated as follows:

> Administrative cost of in-transfer + administrative cost of out-transfer + cost of formal training and orientation + cost of employee surveys or studies + employee transfer expenses + cost of proficiency acquisition X number of employees + administrative cost of special programs.

In addition, the employer has the option of applying (in a nonarbitrary way) different alternatives to different categories of employees; for example, a minimum of two years of service could be set as a requirement for eligibility for the guaranteed minimum of 1,500 hours a year. Another option is to limit the *duration* of coverage; for example, earnings will be protected for six months but, if the business decline goes on longer, they will be reduced gradually.[19]

RECOMMENDATION 2

After balancing the benefits and costs of layoffs and dismissals against those of available alternatives, employers should issue the broadest commitment they can afford with respect to employment security during periods of business decline. They should also declare their intention to broaden the coverage as business success permits, creating an incentive for productivity. In addition, employers should promise that if sacrifices become necessary, they will be shared equitably across the organization.

The chairman of a company noted for high productivity and competitiveness, as well as for its employment security policies, has suggested a hypothetical model for an expandable commitment in the form of goals:

☐ We will now guarantee all people with five years' seniority 2,000 hours of work a year.

☐ We are adopting a business plan which, if achieved, will allow us to extend this to three-year people at the end of two years.

In the meantime, three-year people will be guaranteed 1,840 hours a year.

☐ If we achieve our business plan in two years, people with two years' seniority will be guaranteed 1,840 hours a year.

☐ We will develop a plan this year so that we can schedule easing out obsolete products and plants at a time when the covered employees can be given jobs in new and expanding lines.

☐ We will develop cross-training plans and deferred-maintenance programs so that if regular work is short, people in covered positions can be transferred to other work.

☐ We will revise our performance review program so that the record reflects how well or poorly a person is performing. This reduces the possibility that, during a slack period, employees will be given a discharge for poor performance in place of being laid off temporarily.[20]

The wild card in any commitment to security against long-term declines is always the general business recessions brought on by the federal government's monetary and fiscal policies. Employers can fairly be asked to protect themselves and their employees against long-term declines due to normal market forces, but hardly against those caused by nationwide recessions. In chapter 8 we recommend federal action to help employers fulfill employment security obligations when a general recession makes them unaffordable.

Since employees are usually realistic about the financial limitations of guaranteed employment during a recession, they know that they may need to find a replacement job. In doing so, sufficient lead time and the employer's assistance may be crucial. Thus, we recommend:

Employers should make a written commitment that, in the event that economic recessions make dismissals unavoidable, they will actively assist dismissed employees to find suitable new jobs with other firms.

◀RECOMMENDATION 3

The commitment to employment security is not a one-way street. It should not be conceived as an added cost commitment by the employer without rewards and benefits for the long-term survival of the business. Instead, it must function as a psychological and economic foundation for a competitive company. It should create a partnership, employee involvement, and a high degree of employee commitment to the goals of efficiency, profitability, and quality. This, in the long run, under a climate of trust and earned security, will redound to the mutual benefit of the company, the employees, and the society.

NOTES

1. Bureau of Labor Statistics, U.S. Department of Labor, *Job Tenure Declines as Work Force Changes* (Wasington, D.C.: U.S. Government Printing Office, 1979).

2. R. H. Hayes, "Why Japanese Factories Work," *Harvard Business Review* 59 (July-August 1981): 65.

3. Robert Zager, "Managing Guaranteed Employment," *Harvard Business Review* 56 (May-June 1978): 105-106. When not otherwise identified, all references to Lincoln Electric in this book are based on the above article.

4. Robert N. Beck, "One Company's Strategy at Human Resource Management: A Tradition of Full Employment," *Exchange*, Spring-Summer 1978, p. 22.

5. Fred K. Foulkes, *Personnel Practices in Large Nonunion Companies* (Englewood Cliffs, N.J.: Prentice-Hall, 1980), p. 101.

6. Claire Kolmodin, "Employment Security at Control Data Corporation," an unpublished paper commissioned by Work in America Institute, June 1983.

7. Jocelyn F. Gutchess, *Employment Security in Action: Strategies That Work.* Pergamon Press/Work in America Institute Series (New York: Pergamon Press, 1985).

8. Ibid.

9. W. J. Rowland, "Buick Employe Development Center," an unpublished paper commissioned by Work in America Institute, October 1983.

10. Gutchess, *Employment Security in Action.*

11. Ibid.

12. Ibid.

13. Zager, "Managing Guaranteed Employment," p. 114.

14. Robert Zager, "The Problem of Job Obsolescence: Working It Out at River Works," *Monthly Labor Review* 101 (July 1978): 30.

15. Remarks by members at a meeting of the National Advisory Committee for "Employment Security in a Free Economy," a Work in America Institute policy study, April 19, 1983.

16. Gutchess, *Employment Security in Action.*

17. Remarks by Al Christner, president of United Auto Workers Local 599 in W. J. Rowland, "Buick Employe Development Center," an unpublished paper commissioned by Work in America Institute, October 1983.

18. Dan L. Ward, "The Cost Implications of a No-Layoff Policy," an unpublished paper commissioned by Work in America Institute, January 1984.

19. Ibid.

20. John F. Donnelly, "Strategies and Tactics Leading to Employment Security," an unpublished paper commissioned by Work in America Institute, March 1983.

3.
The Need for
Planning Ahead

The commitment to employment security requires close attention from managers at all levels. The human-resource effects of each planned capital investment or product/marketing change must be calculated early in the game and plans drawn to deal with the consequences. Plans must be readied for the normal swings of business volume and, as far as possible, for macroeconomic business cycles. Every level of management must be involved in planning and executing the human-resource adjustments that ensue.[1]

Leading firms carry out two broad types of planning for employment security:

□ Aggressive planning, to build employment security into the business's strategic plan.

□ Defensive planning, to counter predictable and unpredictable deviations from the strategic plan.

The objective of an aggressive plan is to ensure that the work load proposed for the coming year or years (1) provides the promised minimum number of paid working hours for all protected employees (those to whom the commitment of employment security has been given), and (2) includes a buffer of x percent of additional paid working hours to be performed on overtime or by nonprotected employees. Tactical plans lay out actions to meet the combined work load with as little reliance as possible on overtime or nonprotected employees. These plans will include actions such as cross-training, productivity improvement, and gradual elimination of obsolete products and plants, so that employees can be given jobs in new and expanding lines.

IBM makes plans "to staff at a level below the projected requirements so that, even if the work load falls short of expectations, there will still be a full 40 hours per week for all regular employees. For example, if the workload is projected for 1,000 people during the first quarter of the year, we may choose to staff at a level of 750 people. The difference between projected work load and level of staffing is called a 'buffer,' and it has three major components: overtime, nonregulars, and vendoring."[2] Motorola has adopted a similar approach.

Control Data Corporation has adopted the strategic objective of increasing business to such a point that its current regular work force will be responsible for executing only 70 percent of the work load. The remainder will be met by overtime or "buffers." Some units of the company are shooting to meet 15 percent of the work load through vendoring.[3]

Successful aggressive planning presumes a high degree of reliability in the employer's (1) marketing forecasts, (2) forecasts of productivity growth, (3) forecasts of attrition, and (4) hiring controls, in addition to strong defensive planning capabilities. These are difficult to achieve, but certainly attainable. The choice is clear, however: meet these criteria or incur the cost and lower growth associated with volatile conditions of employment.

Employers should institute a system of planning human-resource needs and deployments as an integral part of the corporate business planning process.  **RECOMMENDATION 4**

Planning Responsibility and Procedure

The effectiveness of a plan depends in large measure on the authority of those who make and execute it. In organizations that take employment security seriously, the planning process starts from the highest levels of authority, makes itself felt at every level, and is reinforced over the years.

The process in IBM has been described by a former senior executive of that company:

> Each operating division is required to prepare a strategic plan that provides broad statistical projections for a period of two to five years and describes in detail the entire busi-

ness plan of the division. This gives division management a long-range look at manpower needs and an opportunity to plan manpower programs. Such things as the training needed to meet new technologies—general skill requirements compared to skills available and employment levels—can be generally assessed. The summary of these plans then provides the corporate staff with an overview of total needs and input needed to develop corporate-wide strategies.

From the long-range strategic plans, each division prepares a much more detailed operating plan, usually for a two-year period. The operating plan becomes the working tool (and measuring device) that the division uses to determine the adequacy of its personnel resources.[4]

During the 1975-76 recession, all hiring required the approval of the Corporate Resource Group, which included the heads of manufacturing, finance, marketing, development, service, and personnel. At Control Data Corporation, the process also shows top-level involvement, although at an earlier stage of development:

A Job Security Task Force was formed by the CEO during the summer of 1980 and chartered to develop and implement a strategy for the maintenance of employment. The major product of the JSTF is the "Rings of Defense" strategy. . . . The task force completed its work during the second quarter of 1981 and began the process of implementing the strategy it had articulated. After approximately 6 months of preparation under the new strategy, CD found itself facing the [recession] and was forced to deal immediately with changes to the "inner rings," the permanent part-time and full-time employees. A number of short-term programs were implemented to minimize the impact of the downturn on these people. Specifically, Control Data created a Special Workforce Action Team (SWAT) . . . to provide continuous employment for displaced permanent employees. The SWAT program is funded on a corporate level and is managed by a central staff who have the responsibility for placement of these displaced employees. In addition to offering either temporary or permanent work assignments . . . the SWAT office has contracted out such support services as career counseling and assessment, outplacement services, and retraining. Now that the immediate economic crisis has been weathered, attention has returned to the long-term rebuilding of the outer rings of defense.[5]

No employee of Control Data can be laid off without central office approval. If the work load declines, the operating divisions have to prepare "social impact" statements, identifying all actions being taken to avoid layoffs. Also, they regularly prepare five-year human-resource plans, updated each year and coordinated by the central office.[6]

In Lincoln Electric Company, a much more compact organization than the two giants previously mentioned, managers and supervisors are responsible for planning for employment security in their own areas. In certain cases, they can be held responsible for employment security problems that originate elsewhere. For example, purchasing department managers are held personally accountable if downtime occurs because supplies are not on hand when needed for the manufacturing process.[7]

The George A. Hormel meat-packing firm, which managed a guaranteed annual wage plan for over 40 years, involved all of its departments in the program. "Considerable planning was required," reported a national business periodical, "involving the preparation of detailed work budgets in each department."[8]

Primary responsibility for human-resource planning should be fixed at the highest level of the firm, but all managers should be responsible for detailed human-resource plans in their own areas.

Foreseeing Potential Threats to Security

Threats to employment security emanate from three principal sources:

☐ Significant changes initiated by the employer for the purpose of improving productivity or other aspects of performance.

☐ Temporary reductions of work load due to business downturns.

☐ Permanent reductions of work load due to business downturns.

Employees, as we have pointed out, assign a different degree of responsibility to the employer for each of these causes, and their behavior toward the employer varies accordingly. Different responses by the employer are therefore in order. For present purposes, however, the question is: Can the employer anticipate and plan for threats from these sources? The answer is an unqualified *yes*!

Employers are continually making changes in every aspect of their business in order to meet changes in products, markets, prices, and competition, and every change is likely to cause employment shifts or displacements of some kind. Technological innovations, although the most clear-cut and publicized, are but one of many types of change. Others relate to:

☐ The organization (for example, overlapping departments are merged, with a consequent reduction of management and supervisory positions).

☐ Job design (for example, craftsworkers agree to do work outside their own trade, reducing the total number of these employees required).

☐ Work flow (for example, insurance company claim processors handle all steps in the process, including dealing with clients, instead of handling only a single stage—such as typing claim forms—with consequent savings in total time required).

☐ Product/market (for example, a poorly selling product is dropped and a new product is introduced, requiring many changes in work assignments).

☐ Materials (for example, old-style "tin" cans are replaced by aluminum, which are, in turn, replaced by thin steel; in each case, new equipment is required and jobs are changed).

☐ Quality control (for example, responsibility for quality control is placed directly on line managers, with the result that many jobs in the quality-control department become surplus).

The range of effects of such changes can be extremely broad. A robot may displace a single worker; computerization of a newspaper may displace hundreds of craftsworkers at a stroke. Displacement may result in upgraded skill requirements, a reduction of hours, total elimination of a job, transfer or reassignment, or separation.

In every instance, however, since the initiative comes from the employer, implementation of change is preceded by a valuable period of time, during which the employer (1) studies whether a change is needed, (2) decides what kind of change to make, (3) designs the change in detail, and (4) procures needed equipment, advice, or materials from outside. The greater the impact of the change, the longer the period of preparation and the farther ahead the employer can anticipate the threat of displacements. The critical management skill is to utilize these periods as advance warnings and to apply the time to achieve a smooth transition.

Temporary Reduction of Work Load

Each business has its own unique pattern of fluctuations—seasonal, cyclical, or secular—not necessarily linked to macroeconomic cycles. Shifts in the fashion, agricultural, and airline industries are associated with the seasons; durable goods are affected by interest rates as well as seasons; and so on. The downside of a fluctuation—except when tied to a general recession—rarely lasts longer than three to six months, and the assumption is that, at the end of that period, business volume will return to "normal." That is, roughly the same work force will be needed as before unless, as sometimes happens, the introduction of new technology during the slump reduces the number.

By analyzing its business history, a firm can estimate the probable depth and duration of such downturns with fair accuracy. Lincoln Electric, for example, has determined that its work load rarely rises or falls more than 6 percent from the trend line during a short-term fluctuation. Many companies have similar rules of thumb. Others move from cycle to cycle without a guideline.

The exact timing of a downturn cannot be pinned down. Still, fluctuations do not occur without warning. Order books begin to show signs of change weeks or months before the impact is felt on the shop floor or in the office. An important part of a manager's job is to sense such changes and take appropriate action as early as possible. This avoids the layoffs which occur when planning fails.

Such uncertainty calls for a battery of alternative plans rather than a single plan. For example, how should the firm respond to a downturn of 5 percent? 10 percent? 15 percent? What if it lasts one month? three months? six months? Alternative plans can be framed at leisure and kept in readiness, in the sure knowledge that at *some* point they are bound to be needed.

Permanent Reduction of Work Load

Long-term (six months or more) reductions of work load are usually related to major changes in external economic conditions. The economy goes into a recession; customer preferences change;

populations and industries move, making relocation of the work-place desirable; new processes are introduced, which cannot be accommodated in current workplaces; new technology makes an existing process and its attendant jobs obsolete; strong competition, domestic or foreign, chops away part of the firm's market share; and inventory builds up, signaling an impending cut in production.

None of these events happen overnight. Aside from general recessions, which are beyond the control of any employer (but also can be anticipated), alert managers can detect signs of change long before they reach the stage at which action must be taken. And following the determination to act comes a long period of study and planning to cope with the emergency. For example, setting up a new process or introducing new technology on any scale rarely takes less than six months; orderly phasing out of part or all of a workplace takes months; moving to a new location takes months or even years. An employer committed to employment security has plenty of time to plan for dealing with the impact of a long-term reduction of work load. However, these lead times often evaporate as management concentrates on the change in production or sales, with delayed—or last-minute—attention to the hard facts on staffing levels. An integrated plan can help management avoid this pitfall.

What Can Be Planned in Advance?

The following chapters will discuss a wide variety of policies and programs to counter threats to employment security. When programs or policies are executed, they affect particular individuals and work units, but it is usually impractical to designate them in advance. What can usefully be done in advance is to (1) list an array of possible responses, (2) study the elements of each response, (3) devise a formula for costing each response, and (4) work out a procedure for determining which combination of responses and trade-offs is most cost-effective against any given threat. These multiple scenarios provide a set of alternative responses tailored to different situations.

This flexible approach reduces to a minimum the amount of scrambling to be done when a threat actually occurs and maximizes the probability of well-considered solutions. It situates the company in a controlling role, managing events, instead of in a reactive posture, manipulated by events.

For example, General Telephone and Electronics has begun a

computerized procedure that enables local managers to estimate rapidly the most cost-effective mix of measures for responding to a surplus (or a shortage) of work force.

A local manager may vary the formula to suit local conditions, but its mere availability constitutes a valuable short-cut. The manager also receives a narrative description of what each alternative may mean for morale, labor relations, community relations, and other visible-but-difficult-to-quantify costs. The provision of intelligent options, combined with more time to choose, increases the options for a cost-effective decision. [9]

Early Warnings

In order to get the most out of having plans in readiness when employment security is threatened, the employer should assign to someone the responsibility for continually scanning the environment for early warning signs. As a rule, everyone and no one is responsible for this duty—a sure-fire way to lose the initiative.

The vice-president for human resources, or the equivalent, is probably best positioned for the assignment, being the one most directly concerned (next to the CEO) with the best use of the work force as a whole. For this purpose the vice-president needs early, reliable information about financial, marketing, and operating plans, as well as personnel reports. Regular attendance at top-level planning meetings would provide access to this information. Vice-presidents for human resources are increasingly being brought in on such deliberations, although this has not always been the case. Their participation in planning is a critical requirement rather than an executive privilege and should become standard practice.

Since every significant challenge to employment security can be anticipated far in advance, employers should use this period to ensure that their responses are ready to execute at the appropriate time.

Another potential source of early warnings is the presence of a senior union official at meetings of senior managers or of the board of directors. The Big Three auto makers, starting with Chrysler, have begun to institutionalize this practice. The Bell System and others are also preparing to do so. Even if managers miss the signals, the ultrasensitive antennae of union leaders can be relied on to vibrate if there is even a distant threat to security. For example, soon after the president of the UAW became a director of Chrysler, the company's board formed a five-member committee charged with insuring that when a plant has to be closed "every possible action is taken to alleviate the impact on the workers, the community in which the plant is located, and the government units involved." The UAW presence in the boardroom assured the committee's success.[10]

These high-level union-management meetings could include:

☐ General operations and business development of the firm.

☐ Matters of mutual interest, involving government relations.

☐ The industry's human-resource needs, trends, developments, and concepts.

☐ Matters of general administration.

☐ Product development, sales, and marketing programs.

☐ Commissioned studies on matters of mutual interest.

☐ Joint visits to learn from other companies and organizations.

A Union Role in Planning

The fact that union advice has proved helpful in the corporate boardroom suggests that employers committed to employment security should consider involving the union in developing advance plans to meet that commitment. While no employer will want to give the union veto power or the right to dictate policy, many may want to consult it on such matters and develop planning as a joint process.

When an actual threat arises and detailed plans have to be prepared and executed, union involvement is practically indispensable. Here, the question is not whether to transfer decisions to unions, but rather to create a working partnership. The union is interested in corporate survival and growth. The more the union knows and the earlier it knows it, the greater the level of understanding and the broader the options for participation and cooperation. Some of the UAW's joint planning efforts with Ford and GM are best-case examples of remarkable progress.

RECOMMENDATION 7

On all matters affecting employment security, the CEO should regularly consult with senior local and international officers of the union and should invite the union as early as possible to join in designing and executing responsive measures.

NOTES

1. Materials Research Corporation of Orangeburg, New York—one of the few firms candid enough to describe the consequences of neglecting to plan—followed an unannounced policy of no layoffs for over 15 years. In the late 1970s it took the bold step of spelling out the commitment in its employee handbook. Since the business had been on a steady growth course, no thought was given to planning for possible adversity, and the recession of 1981-1983 caught the company unprepared. Management improvised a series of painful and costly responses, which left the company bruised but with its commitment intact. Based on a case study in Jocelyn F. Gutchess, *Employment Security in Action: Strategies That Work.* Pergamon Press/Work in America Institute Series (New York: Pergamon Press, 1985).

2. Robert N. Beck, "One Company's Strategy at Human Resource Management: A Tradition of Full Employment," *Exchange,* Spring-Summer 1978, p. 22.

3. Claire Kolmodin, "Employment Security at Control Data Corporation," an unpublished paper commissioned by Work in America Institute, June 1983.

4. Beck, "One Company's Strategy at Human Resource Management," p. 22, 23.

5. Kolmodin, "Employment Security at Control Data Corporation."

6. Jocelyn F. Gutchess, *Employment Security in Action: Strategies That Work.* Pergamon Press/Work in America Institute Series (New York: Pergamon Press, 1985).

7. Robert Zager, "Managing Guaranteed Employment," *Harvard Business Review* 56 (May-June 1978): 109-110.

8. Robert S. Eckley, "Company Action to Stabilize Employment," *Harvard Business Review* 44 (July-August 1966): 54-55.

9. Dan L. Ward, "The Cost Implications of a No-Layoff Policy," an unpublished paper commissioned by Work in America Institute, January 1984.

10. John Hoerr, "A Union Seat on the Board: The Test Isn't Over," *Business Week,* November 22, 1982, p. 30.

4.
Lean Staffing

Since it is always easier and more pleasant to offer a job than to take it away, employers naturally tend to let the work force grow faster than the work load. When the surplus becomes too large to ignore, either because the work load has dwindled or competition has intensified, there is likely to be overreaction with a vengeance.

Therefore, employers committed to employment security learn to reinforce their corporate programs to avoid the creation of surpluses in the first place. They adopt four principal lines of attack: (1) long-term work-load plans are linked to authorized work-force levels to ensure that the number of protected employees does not exceed the amount necessary to meet the *long-term growth* of work load; (2) hiring and firing practices ensure that protected employees are, and remain, competent to meet the needs of the organization; (3) annual operating plans provide sufficient flexibility to meet short-term fluctuations of work load, without adding protected employees; (4) production, marketing, and financial policies minimize the need for sudden ups and downs in the size of the protected work force.

RECOMMENDATION 8

Since the accumulation of surplus employees in prosperous times can undermine management efforts to maintain employment security in hard times, employers should ensure that (1) authorized work-force levels are tied to long-term work-load

*plans; (2) employees are competent to meet the changing needs
of the organization; (3) annual operating plans can accommodate
short-term increases of work load without adding protected
employees; and (4) production, marketing, and financial policies
help to avoid sudden changes in work-force levels.*

CONTROLLING GROWTH OF THE
PROTECTED WORK FORCE

The previous chapter describes how long-range work-load and
work-force requirements can be combined in a single package.
Since the forecasting of long-term work-force requirements is as
much art as science, employers committed to employment security take strong measures to hold the number of protected employees to the minimum.

☐ In Lincoln Electric, orders to add new employees emanate
directly from the president and CEO. The company waits until
the pressure of foreseeable demand exceeds what can be met by
stretching the existing work force through greater effort and
overtime. This may penalize the company in the rare case when
the industry as a whole experiences a spurt of orders.[1]

☐ At 3M, "lean staffing" is considered good for morale
because employees never have to kill time.[2]

☐ Wyeth Labs also subscribes to leanness, but warns that
excessive leanness—especially in the case of professional skills
that cannot easily be augmented by subcontractors or temporaries—can handicap efforts to develop new products.[3]

☐ "The IBM corporate staff approves all hiring to fill authorized work force levels, although the level of control varies,
depending on the sensitivity of the environment. In high-growth
times, the filling of approved staff plans may be delegated to the
division presidents. When there are signs of business uncertainty,
however, hiring may be reviewed by the corporate staff quarterly,
monthly, or even on an individual-hire basis. During the 1975-76
recession, all hiring required corporate approval. A Corporate
Resource Group, including the staff heads of manufacturing,
finance, marketing, development, service, and personnel, was
formed. The group continually reviewed the personnel status and
projections of each division and then directed divisions and locations in need of people to those divisions and locations with

surpluses. Internal recruiting programs were reviewed for adequacy, and only when the group was satisfied that all internal sources were exhausted was external hiring authorized." The group continued in operation even after the recession ended.[4]

Each work unit in an organization should maintain a staffing standard, against which requests for permission to hire should be evaluated. The standard itself should be periodically reviewed and revised in the light of changing work loads, new technology, new products or services, turnover, learning curve, and so on. Some employers sharpen the standards by setting annual productivity improvement goals. At Lincoln Electric, additional pressure is generated by the employees, whose individual and plant-wide incentive payments are inversely proportional to the number of sharers.

Toyota has a crunch method of setting standards:

> Normally you don't want workers or machines to be idle, so you keep on producing parts whether you need them in the assembly stage or not. But if you do that in the just-in-time system, there is no place to stack them. If the workers have the materials to make parts but no place to stack them, they have to stop producing. When that happens, the supervisor knows that he has too many people working on that production stage, and the workers realize there are more people on the job than necessary.[5]

ENSURING THAT PROTECTED EMPLOYEES ARE COMPETENT TO MEET THE EMPLOYER'S NEED

If hiring and firing are to be held to the minimum, employment security firms must make sure that permanent employees are, and will remain, competent to meet the organization's needs in the future. Companies take special care to hire people with the requisite capabilities and to weed out promptly those who do not perform up to standard; they develop flexibility for varying assignments, through training, retraining, and the incentive of pay-for-knowledge; and they promote from within whenever it is reasonable to do so. Employees respond in kind.

Hiring for Permanency

Successful employment security firms hire with exceptional care because they expect their employees to commit themselves to a career. The fact that the firms usually have many more applicants than vacancies, even during prosperous times, enhances their ability to be selective. This selectivity creates a better fit between the job, the company, and the employee, and tends to prolong the relationship.

At Lincoln Electric, each recruit, after screening, is interviewed by three senior company officers, who assess his or her capacity for growth, among other things. Then the recruit observes the job to be filled and is interviewed by the supervisor in charge. If the supervisor approves and the match is made, the new employee undergoes two years of probation before becoming permanent.[6]

Flexible Assignments

Since the organization's needs are always in flux, an employment security firm can staff "lean" only if employees are flexible and capable of being moved with good results from one job to another. Flexibility implies not only competence to perform various jobs, but willingness to be moved. This is common to all experienced exponents of employment security. A highly visible example is Delta Air Lines, whose unionized pilots have been known to handle baggage and to staff ticket counters when necessary. Many of its pilots also made sales calls on customers when flight schedules were curtailed in the 1973 oil embargo. A recent agreement at American Airlines has brought similar flexibility to its unionized ground employees.

In some cases, earnings are protected in full when such moves occur. In others, there may be gradual reduction to a lower-rated wage. At Lincoln Electric, the employee immediately receives an adjustment to the base rate normal for the new job assignment.

Training and retraining are crucial for flexibility, especially when technological change is rapid. IBM's programs are justly famous in this respect; between 1974 and 1976 the company shifted 5,000 employees to new positions, and 2,000 of them had to learn new skills.

General Motors and Ford, pursuant to their 1982 agreements with the UAW, have set up security-oriented training programs jointly managed by company and union. AT&T and the Communications Workers of America (CWA) agreed in 1983 to inaugurate a similar program by August 1984. These programs are discussed more fully below:

□ Although the auto programs have been mainly concerned with retraining for laid-off employees who will not be recalled, they have also turned their attention to current workers. The Ford agreement created a National Development and Training Center to arrange or provide training "to upgrade/sharpen present job skills, and provide updating on state-of-the-art technology for skilled and semiskilled employees, based on present and anticipated job requirements." The company contributes five cents per employee hour, for an annual budget of $12 million to $15 million. The program offers: prepaid tuition assistance for formal education and training, subject to a cap of $1,000 a year; career and educational guidance and counseling; education in, and enhancement of, basic skills; and specially tailored college-level associate degree programs.[7]

☐ The General Motors arrangement is basically similar to Ford's. However, the Buick/Flint division has carried the idea a step further with its Employe Development Center. Every worker displaced by a production change (see chapter 2) is entitled to a minimum of one year in the center, with full pay protection, to acquire new skills that will be useful to the division.[8]

☐ Each major unit of the Bell System has agreed to develop a job-displacement training program that will help workers qualify for anticipated job vacancies within the company if their present jobs are terminated or downgraded; provide early notice of potential job terminations; and offer training for anticipated vacancies. The training will take place outside of working hours and be unpaid. In addition, the Bell units will establish career development training programs (also unpaid and outside of working hours) that will help employees prepare for career opportunities or job changes within the company; be "generic" rather than "job-specific"; cover technical, sales, clerical, and other functional skills; and be taken into account by the employer when employees are being considered for promotion or transfer.[9]

☐ Communications Workers of America (CWA) initiated a jointly funded technological-skill testing program in 1982 for the purpose of matching employee skills with employer needs throughout the communications industry. Members, for a small fee, were tested in basic electronics, solid state, digital, and other technologies. Those who failed could obtain additional training, while those who passed received a certificate recognized by employers in the industry.[10]

Training for new technology involves not just training but the context within which training occurs. For example, has management given sufficient advance notice of change? Has it fully disclosed the nature of the new technology, its purposes, and its impact on the workplace? Is the integrity of the bargaining unit affected? What will the change do to wages, classifications, and seniority? These questions should be considered by a joint employer-union committee.

Lastly, training can increase employees' flexibility by acquainting them with such basics as the firm's organizational structure, product lines, production technology, and competition. The vast majority of American workers are quite ignorant of these facts, and most have never even had a guided tour of the site in which they work!

When employment security is absent, jobs splintered, and people dismissed in large numbers, as is traditional in smokestack America, unions view *in*flexibility as essential to self-defense. When employers inch toward more flexible modes of production, such as semiautonomous work teams, however, they find the unions ready to accommodate them. Pay-for-knowledge has been negotiated by the United Auto Workers, United Steelworkers of America, and the International Union of Electrical Workers as a proper form of payment for cross-training. The team member moves up the wage scale with each additional skill mastered; top rate is paid to any member who learns all the skills applied by the team. Part of the quid pro quo, when a traditional plant changes to team operation, is a guarantee to union members that the transition will cause no one to be dismissed or downgraded.

Dealing with Poor Performers

Care in hiring and training is necessary, but not sufficient to ensure that employees retain the flexibility and competence the employer needs. Not even a lengthy probation is foolproof. A certain number of employees do not perform as expected, for reasons not always apparent to their bosses. Their continued presence in the firm harms the cause of employment security because (1) it requires the firm to hire additional employees who should not be needed, and (2) it tempts management to devise general layoffs and/or early-retirement schemes as a cover for pushing them out.

The most effective antidote for such slippage is rigorous performance appraisal, conducted with as much objectivity as the situation allows. Few managers enjoy appraising their subordinates; fewer do it well. Yet, despite their reluctance, it must be done. Managers should be required to appraise employees at regular intervals and, in that connection, to recommend training, retraining, transfer, promotion, or dismissal. Employees who are considered to be irredeemably unsatisfactory should be removed, with due process, as soon as possible. Vacillation injures employee and employer alike and may also expose the employer to legal problems when dismissal finally occurs.

Typically, employment security firms rely heavily on promotion from within. Promotability thus becomes a key quality to look for in selecting a new employee. Thereafter, the firm does not go outside to fill any vacancy until it has determined that the qualifications cannot be met—even with additional training—by current employees. (This procedure offers employees additional forms of employment security—career and lateral-move security.)

Lincoln Electric gives frequent merit ratings to every employee, not only as a factor in bonus sharing but also as a means of bringing promotable talent to light. Selection, prompt appraisals, and promotions from within work in effective combination to increase employment opportunity and security. They increase productivity as well.

Every work unit in an organization should establish, by agreement with top management, tough but realistic staffing standards. If the work unit wants to add employees in excess of the standard, it should have to obtain top management permission. Adherence to standard is facilitated if (1) all new hires are regarded as career employees; (2) all protected employees are, by agreement, willing and able to be deployed in a wide variety of assignments; (3) unsatisfactory performers are brought up to standard, reassigned, or dismissed early in their careers.

MEETING TEMPORARY WORK-LOAD INCREASES WITHOUT ADDING PROTECTED EMPLOYEES

Employers committed to employment security also learn to meet temporary increases of work load—which, as J.F. Lincoln of Lincoln Electric pointed out, are inevitable—without adding to the number of *protected* employees. They do so by the use of "buffers." Some employ intracompany resources (overtime, internal recruiting), while others engage outside resources (subcontractors/vendors, temporaries). As noted earlier, IBM and Control Data do more than that: they factor such buffers into their annual operating plans (revised monthly), setting a definite percentage of the expected normal work load to be performed by these resources. Thus, if work load falls off during the year, protected employees continue to have full assignments. IBM's typewriter division estimated that by the judicious use of buffers it could avoid surpluses of protected employees, even if "expected normal demand" fell as much as 25 percent. When demand exceeds the norm, temporary employees are hired or emergency overtime is used.

Intracompany Resources

Various resources inside the organization can be tapped by companies when the work load temporarily exceeds the capacity of protected employees to perform the work. Among these are the use of overtime, borrowing employees from other work sites, and other means.

Overtime. Overtime is the buffer most commonly used by U.S. employers to cope with temporary work-load increases, for the simple reason that it is cheaper to pay regular employees premium rates for a while than to hire, train, and fire new people.

Problems arise with regard to how much, and for how long, overtime should be used. In principle, one hour of overtime a day increases output by 12.5 percent. Increasing overtime causes fatigue and personal problems, however, which lead to diminishing returns. Day-after-day overtime aggravates these problems. If overtime becomes habitual, it engenders the "British disease," in which employees readjust their living standards and become dependent on the extra income.

In nonunion employment security companies, overtime is usually mandatory. For example:

☐ IBM operating plans are based on an understanding that employees will work at least 10 to 12 Saturdays a year, and as many as 22 if necessary.[11]

☐ Lincoln Electric workers like a few hours of overtime a week, but object if it goes beyond that. However, during the annual summer rush, there may be a series of 50-hour weeks.

Fifty-hour weeks also occur occasionally at other times, when they are unavoidable.[12]

Note the significant difference of approach between IBM and Lincoln Electric. IBM, which is committed to "full employment," plans overtime as part of the hours needed to meet expected normal demand. Lincoln, which guarantees not less than 30 hours of work per week for the 49 workweeks of the year, plans short weeks to meet a fall-off in demand. In each case, management and employees (and their union) have to decide which approach is preferable.

Unionized workers like voluntary overtime as much as nonunion workers do. *Mandatory* overtime is another matter, as the UAW/International Harvester strike of 1979 so painfully demonstrated. Since unions usually deal with companies that are *not* committed to employment security, they fight to limit overtime in order to keep more members at work, or to force managements to recall members on layoff. They pose tough questions to the employer:

☐ Is excessive overtime being scheduled because it is cheaper to pay premium rates than to recall employees?

☐ Is all the equipment already in use, leaving no openings for recalled or new employees?

☐ Is the situation truly an emergency?

☐ Is the overtime designed to meet a short-run rise in sales, or are long-term prospects good enough to warrant acquiring new equipment and employees?

If employers were committed to employment security and willing to consult on the appropriateness of mandatory overtime, unions would likely take a distinctly less hostile position on the question.

The use of permanent part-time employees can make overtime a much more flexible instrument. In one employment security firm, one-third of the work force consists of permanent part-timers. Thus, by changing the part-time schedules rapidly from 20 hours per week to 32, the firm is able to raise total work-force hours per week by 12 percent.[13]

Borrowing Employees. In multisite companies, especially where work sites are not too distant from one another, it may be feasible for one with a shortage of employees to borrow temporarily from one with a surplus. Except during general recessions, different sites normally have different cycles of demand.

As mentioned earlier, IBM makes extensive use of internal recruiting, and not only for blue-collar people. In one case, "the Office Products Division (OPD) had a need for additional marketing representatives (salespeople). At the same time, several plants in other divisions had light work loads and too much personnel. When the [Corporate Resource Group] identified the imbalance, it prescribed internal recruiting. As a result, OPD marketing teams visited the plants and held seminars to explain to interested manufacturing people what the available jobs were like. Those who had a further interest were interviewed. In the end, almost 600 people became qualified and accepted marketing jobs in cities throughout the country."[14]

Other Measures. Other measures are used from time to time to meet temporary work-load increases without adding protected employees:

☐ Work may be transferred temporarily within the firm from a site with excess work to one with a shortage. (IBM does this as a last resort.)

☐ An inventory of finished products may be depleted to meet the surge.

☐ Employees scheduled to take holidays or vacations during the push may be asked—or offered rewards—to change their schedules.

External Resources

Sometimes it is necessary during a peak work period to go outside the organization to find means of handling the work. Among these measures are the use of temporary employees and buffer subcontracting.

Temporary Employees. After overtime, temporary employees are probably the buffer most commonly used by employment security companies. Many companies hire them when a new product is being launched or when any other limited-time buildup of employees is needed. Temporaries may be hired for a specific job or for a stated period, typically for periods of 90 days to 12 months.

Some companies engage former regular employees or annuitants as temporary employees—qualified people who have left to raise a family, retired, or resigned for other personal reasons. It is not unusual for individuals—particularly older workers, mothers of young children, or students—to prefer working on a temporary basis because it gives them greater control over their lives. They may take repeated temporary assignments from the same employer.

For one employment security company, the sole source of new hires at the unskilled level are temporaries who have exhibited good attendance and performance. The company provides temporaries with some of the benefits available to regular employees and even includes them in the job-posting system. The question of benefits for temporary workers is of concern to unions and should be given careful thought.

Some observers have suggested that Lincoln Electric's practice of not extending its guarantee to employees with less than two years' service amounts to the creation of de facto temporaries. This is a misinterpretation. Everyone hired by the company is viewed as permanent, subject only to probation; probationers have all the rights of regulars except that of voluntary transfer. Only a small minority are ever asked to leave.

Other critics assert that the extensive use of temporaries by Japanese "lifetime employment" firms serves to create a two-tier work force. A more realistic view would recognize that prior to the introduction of lifetime employment in the late 1950s and early 1960s, few Japanese workers enjoyed employment security. They were employees at will, just as most American workers are today. The achievement of the last generation has been to raise one-third of the Japanese work force to a high degree of security, while the other two-thirds are no worse off than before. In fact, they are better off, because the entire economy has become so much more prosperous as a result of the change.

Buffer Subcontracting. Subcontracting as a buffer must be clearly distinguished from subcontracting in general: the objectives and methods differ fundamentally. Many firms subcontract the parts of their work load that can be done more cost-effectively by outside organizations, without regard to whether the principal firm's permanent employees and plant and equipment are capable of doing it in-house (often, indeed, they do so as a means of cutting back the permanent work force). Such subcontracting, an everyday feature throughout the economy, is subject only to quantity control, on-time delivery, reliability, and collective contract terms.

By contrast, only a handful of U.S. firms use subcontracting as a deliberate buffering mechanism; IBM and Control Data are the best known. The objective of this kind of subcontracting is not to reduce or weaken the existing permanent work force, but to avoid expanding the work force faster than the permanent work load. It serves to ensure that permanent employees will not run out of work if the work load declines. It is essential, therefore, that the work subcontracted as a buffer can be performed in-house by permanent employees and by equipment already at hand if it becomes necessary to bring it back in-house.

The nature of the work suitable for subcontracting as a buffer depends on the individual firm. IBM has subcontracted manufacturing work, for the most part; Control Data has subcontracted software production.

IBM's typewriter division subcontracts about 5 percent of "normal expected demand," in the form of parts, subassemblies, painting, and packaging. At Control Data, each operating unit has been asked to outline the process through which it can move 15 percent of its work into subcontracting as the business grows. One manufacturing division plans to reach 30 percent buffer subcontracting by the end of 1984. Control Data's managers, as part of the change, will (1) establish cost trade-offs between subcontracting and internal expansion, (2) consolidate vendor contracts where possible, and (3) identify interdivisional opportunities for retrieving work.

IBM's continuous programs of training for all employees and its policy of rotation equip employees to perform many different tasks. Thus, they can readjust quickly when subcontracted work is brought back in during slack periods.[15] Control Data requires its managers to ensure, before letting subcontracts, that their employees have—or could be cost-effectively trained to have—the skills to take work back in-house.[16]

Both companies recognize an obligation to the firms that accept buffer subcontracting. They make clear beforehand that the work is subject to being withdrawn in case of a slump. They do not let their orders assume too large a proportion of any subcontractor's order book. And they try to spread their subcontracting over a wide geographical area to prevent a cascading of unemployment.

Several objections to buffer subcontracting have been raised:

1. Can it be justified economically? If an outside firm can do the work more economically, there must be some loss when the work is brought back (and the loss is aggravated because the

principal firm would then be under pressure). On the other hand, if the outside firm cannot do the work as economically, the principal firm sustains a loss until it brings the work back.

The flaw in this argument is that it seeks to evaluate buffer subcontracting in isolation. A firm uses buffer subcontracting only as a means to the end of employment security. The cost of subcontracting must therefore be evaluated against the costs of other alternatives, such as expanding the protected work force or hiring temporaries, and also against the benefits of employment security.

2. Will unions accept it? Unions have consistently opposed subcontracting where the expected effect is to undercut their bargaining position or to transfer work from union to nonunion hands. Since buffer subcontracting does not reduce the protected work force—in fact, it strengthens its protection—the union's bargaining position may be different. At Bethlehem Steel's Johnstown, Pennsylvania, plant, for example, the United Steelworkers agreed to relax restrictions on contracting out mechanical work in exchange for lifetime job security. The agreement also allows the company to move skilled trades workers to other jobs when no work in their regular assignments is available.[17]

If a local union believes that its mission is to expand membership regardless of employment security, it will resist buffer subcontracting, but such attitudes are being challenged by the high demand for employment security among American workers.

The more difficult issue relates to the possibility of work going to nonunion lower-paid workers outside. On this point there is no substitute for negotiations between employer and union.

3. Does buffer subcontracting merely shift insecurity from one group of workers to another? Not entirely, but to some degree. Both IBM and Control Data, as noted, try to minimize this possibility by geographical dispersion of subcontractors and by limiting the amount of work given to any one of them. IBM encourages its subcontractors to practice employment security themselves and to create their own buffers. But companies that plan as assiduously as IBM and Control Data should go a step further. They should give the subcontractor sufficient advance notice—three to six months seems feasible—before taking the contract back in-house. This would allow any businesslike subcontractor to make some provision for the security of its employees, except, possibly, in a general recession.

How to Manage Employment Security: Staffing Strategies

When companies seek employment security for their employees, they plan ahead for adverse business conditions, but *keep their work force lean the year round* by

Matching work-force levels to long-term demand

☐

Hiring employees with special
attention to competence

☐

Encouraging flexibility by training employees
to fill a variety of jobs

☐

Appraising employee performance frequently
and taking appropriate action

☐

Meeting temporary work-load increases without
adding permanent employees, by using

overtime

temporary employees

subcontracting

transfers of employees from units with
smaller work loads

☐

Stabilizing demand

☐

Using flexible production methods

Buffer subcontracting need not be a macroeconomic zero-sum game either. Insofar as employment security enables a firm to become more productive than it would be otherwise, it increases competitiveness and the wealth of society at any given level of demand, even in a general recession. (For example, the success of IBM and Hewlett-Packard, which is in no small measure due to employment security, helped create a huge new industry with hundreds of thousands of good jobs.) During nonrecessionary periods, the principal firm may suffer a slump while other industries are busy; or one division of the firm may be in a slump while others are busy. It does not automatically follow that the withdrawal of a subcontract causes unemployment, even temporarily. However, the fact remains that the subcontractor is always more vulnerable to business conditions.

"Buffers"—such as overtime, transfers of people or work load, temporary employees, and subcontracting—can help greatly in maintaining employment security in the face of short-term business fluctuations. At the same time, buffers may cause unwanted side-effects. Employers should, therefore, use them in accordance with clear ground rules agreed upon with employees and local and international unions.

STABILIZING THE WORK LOAD

Sharp fluctuations of business volume make it hard to avoid the cycle of hiring and firing. Therefore, employment security firms use various marketing and production strategies to help stabilize the work load. They are not content to remain static in a dynamic economy but, instead, reach out to counteract adverse conditions with more aggressive strategies.

Marketing

On the marketing side, the dominant strategies are to (1) stabilize demand, (2) launch products with deliberate speed, (3) avoid reliance on a single market or customer, and (4) maintain growth at a sustainable rate.

Stabilizing Demand. Eastman Kodak, one of the earliest practitioners of employment security, also led in the development of sales forecasting and inventory control as methods of leveling out seasonal demand. Short-range and long-range forecasts, frequently updated, provided the basis for production schedules and inventory plans. The company continued its employment security policy until the late 1970s, when it became sluggish because of its long domination of the industry. As a result, it fell prey to foreign competition and lost market share too fast to absorb its surplus workers.[18]

Procter & Gamble, another early 1920s exponent of sales forecasting, reorganized its distribution system at that time in tandem with the adoption of employment security. Guaranteeing 48 weeks of work a year for a large proportion of its employees, Procter & Gamble began selling directly to retailers. This countered the tendency of wholesalers to buy and stockpile goods when prices were low or special promotions were offered, practices which amplified fluctuations of demand. The company also directed greater marketing efforts toward customers who kept up a steady flow of orders.[19]

Levi Strauss, for similar reasons, recently decided to market its products through Sears Roebuck and J.C. Penney.

Another employment security company found that by offering attractive leasing options to customers, it created a steadier flow of orders than was possible by selling outright. The policy contributed to both sales and security.

Launching Products with Deliberate Speed. Some full-employment companies, especially high-tech firms, refuse to enter the market with a new product that is superior technically, but whose reliability is untested. For example, they do not wish to see their market share peak at 15 percent and then fall below 8 percent when they could have grown slowly to roughly 35 percent of the market. They prefer a six-month delay in introduction to iron out the bugs. Seldom first in the market with new products, they purposely lag behind the state of the art by a year or two.

Digital Equipment, for example, reports that it lets its leading-edge users (such as government research labs) push them into the development of new products. Hewlett-Packard, too, has been described as a "counter puncher." When a competitor's new product comes on the market, Hewlett-Packard engineers ask their customers what they like or dislike about the new products while servicing Hewlett-Packard equipment. Soon Hewlett-Packard sales people are calling on customers with a new product that answers customer needs more exactly than the competitor's. The result, the company reports, is satisfied and loyal customers.

IBM also learns from others' mistakes. It is rarely the first to take a new technical step and, time after time, its new lines are better designed and more efficiently marketed as, for example, the PC II personal computer. In the very early stages of product introduction, IBM also makes a conscious effort to maximize customer satisfaction in such areas as parts, service, warranty, operator training, maintenance, and delivery.

The strategy here is that a well-engineered, well-tested product, delivered on time and backed up with prompt shipment of repair parts, will survive long after the introduction of a new technology and new features. This measured approach to the market-place, which supports long-term growth, is more prevalent in well-established high-tech companies. Newer entrants to the field, such as Tandem and Intel, try a "first-with-the-best" approach in well-defined market niches. As high-tech companies experience slowed growth and mature, however, this approach may not be the most appropriate strategy for long-term profitability and employment stability.

Avoiding Reliance on a Single Market or Customer. An employment security firm cannot afford to be overreliant on a single market or customer. Some make it a point to sell their products simultaneously in several markets, whose differing characteristics make it unlikely that all will fluctuate in the same way or at the same time.

In order to avoid the effects of variations in government contracts upon the stability of employment, some companies limit the amount of government business they undertake. For example, for many years Gorman-Rupp, a manufacturer of pumps, has limited its government sales to a certain percentage of its total business. Commenting on this, James Gorman, company president, said:

> We try as best we can to look two years ahead to see what is going to happen to the various industries which we serve. In the current situation, we determined several years ago that things did not look too rosy and, as a result, made a determination that more military government business

would be needed. In the past, we had arbitrarily limited our government sales to 5 percent of the total but in this case we had adjusted it upward to between 12 percent and 15 percent and, quite honestly, are glad we did.[20]

Early in its corporate history, Hewlett-Packard rejected a large government contract for reasons of employment stability. Reflecting on the company's early approach, an officer of the company stated:

> When we were small, we were given an opportunity to take on a $7 million contract. Now, this was completely out of our bracket. To accomplish that sort of thing meant hiring a lot of people, and later firing them at the end of the contract. In thinking about this, it was clear that it would affect not only the temporary people but also those who were permanent. They would know that anytime we saw an opportunity to make money we would grab it regardless of the results on people.
>
> Instead, the philosophy has been that when you come to work at Hewlett-Packard we hope we are offering you a permanent job. You do your work well and we will provide the employment. So we turned the contract down, even though it probably would have made a lot of money.[21]

Employment security clearly was an essential part of Hewlett-Packard's strategy—so much so that it turned down a lucrative contract rather than alter its basic philosophy. Other companies also are known to avoid large government contracts for the same reason.

Finally, some companies, including Hewlett-Packard, are careful to select government contracts for items that are closely allied to their regular off-the-shelf products. Often an initial government request for a product will list a hundred or more different specifications. Hewlett-Packard will then deliberately negotiate with government contractors to reduce the number of specifications and streamline products in an attempt to duplicate—or come close to duplicating—a product the company is currently manufacturing. In some cases, this process results in modifications of the government's requirements; in other cases, it results in the rejection of a government contract by Hewlett-Packard.

A number of companies give careful attention to their dependence on particular customers. For example, one company made special efforts to reduce its dependence on Sears Roebuck as a customer. The president of another company stated:

> From the beginning we wanted a diverse customer group because, for our own security, we did not want to be dependent on any specific customers or sectors of the economy. [22]

This company sells to over 400,000 firms, with no single customer accounting for over .05 percent of sales.

Maintaining Growth at a Sustainable Rate. Employment security firms vary greatly in size of revenue and work force, but many share a policy of aggressive but carefully paced pursuit of growth. Critics often question the replicability of employment security on the ground that it is found mainly in rapidly growing companies, where shortages rather than surpluses of workers are the rule. In fact, the main growth of many of these companies—such as IBM, Hewlett-Packard, Digital Equipment, Lincoln Electric, Delta Air Lines, People Express, Federal Express, and Nucor—occurred *after* they adopted employment security. Conversely, the enormous growth of the automotive industry produced a totally opposite policy.

Overrapid growth, of course, can be destabilizing. Long lead times are required for expansion, hiring, and inventory, so an unexpected deceleration can wreak havoc, as so often happens in the microelectronics industry. Steady long-term growth, on the other hand, requires high-quality and/or low-cost production, and employment security contributes to both.

Full-employment companies in the business of transporting people or cargo display similar marketing strategies. Federal Express, Delta Air Lines, and People Express are the low-cost producers in their markets and have pioneered the concept of unique central hubs for their industries. These central sorting facilities help to ensure reliability for shipments and allow the companies more flexibility in the use of equipment and personnel. All three companies moved rapidly to market domination in the early stages of their business, and have expanded the definition and nature of the markets in which they participate. For example, Federal Express has dramatically enlarged the demand for rapid delivery. People Express has managed to increase the number of people selecting air travel as their mode of transportation, at the expense of rail, bus, and automobile travel. People Express is now second only to Eastern Airlines in landings in the New York metropolitan area.

The concept of market expansion and market domination is not new to full employment companies. Bank of America dominates the California banking market. IBM is preeminent in several aspects of the computer market. And Procter & Gamble has dominated and expanded various parts of the consumer-products market for years.

Lincoln Electric drove itself to give customers more and more for less and less, each year offering existing products at lower constant-dollar prices, and improved products at last year's constant-dollar prices, even while the constant-dollar price of steel—its principal ingredient—soared. Gradually, Lincoln Electric outdistanced the field, and some of the largest enterprises in the country dropped out of the competition. A *New York Times* article of January 15, 1984 stated that Lincoln Electric "has, in large part, driven competitors like Westinghouse and General Electric from the arc welding business. So secure is the company in its niche that, for all practical purposes, Lincoln *is* the arc welding business."[23]

Chaparral Steel, IBM, Nucor, and Quill, among others, demonstrate the advantages of being the low-cost producers in their industries. Both Chaparral and Nucor, steel producers, gained market share during economic downturns.

Production

On the production side, flexibility is the keynote: flexibility of personnel skills and time, plant use, technology, and material inputs. An official of one employment security firm recently said: "We don't dedicate plants to products but rather to processes. And we have a very centralized material resource planning system."[24] At another firm, "all manufacturing is dedicated to multiple products."[25]

The value of flexible technology was recently illustrated at John Deere & Company, whose new capital equipment enables it to process totally different components by simply reprogramming the machines and modifying them somewhat. The company says it now can make aircraft parts or washing machine parts or almost anything within a certain size range. John Deere has set up an internal group to seek out defense and other nontraditional business to take advantage of this versatility. New technology has also allowed General Motors, Motorola, and Fairchild Camera and Instrument to bring back to the United States thousands of jobs which they had previously exported to low-wage countries overseas.

Other firms seek stability by avoiding dependence on particular materials and suppliers. Some have adapted to a diversity of fuels—natural gas, coal, or oil. Some can switch their processing from one raw material to another, or can produce different product mixes.

Lincoln Electric, which pioneered "just-in-time" inventory control years ago, holds its purchasing department managers responsible for the timely delivery of materials. The costs arising from late deliveries are charged against the department's merit ratings and annual bonuses. For each material, the department has to find alternative suppliers with low prices and high reliability. In exchange, the company is a highly reliable, year-round customer, running continually despite most external fluctuations, and paying bills quickly enough to take a cash discount.

RECOMMENDATION 11 *Firms seeking to stabilize their work loads for the sake of employment security should focus on (1) stabilizing the flow of orders, (2) maintaining growth at a sustainable rate, (3) avoiding overdependency on a single market or customer, and (4) achieving flexibility in the use of production personnel, plant, process, and materials.*

Every organization allowed to follow its natural bent will become obese. But obesity and employment security cannot co-exist except in a monopoly or a near-monopoly. The general run of firms, those which compete for a living, must exercise unremitting self-discipline. They can accomplish this by:

☐ Setting and keeping lean staffing standards.

☐ Aligning the growth of the work force with the long-term growth of work load.

☐ Cultivating flexibility in their employees.

☐ Designing annual operating plans that can meet short-term increases of work load without adding protected employees.

☐ Adopting production, marketing, and financial policies that avert the need for sudden hirings and firings.

NOTES

1. Robert Zager, "Managing Guaranteed Employment," *Harvard Business Review* 56 (May-June 1978): 103-115.

2. Howard J. Sanders, "Employers Tell How to Avoid Layoffs," *Chemical and Engineering News*, December 3, 1973, pp. 13-17.

3. Ibid.

4. Robert N. Beck, "One Company's Strategy at Human Resource Management: A Tradition of Full Employment," *Exchange*, Spring-Summer 1978, p. 23.

5. Toyota Motor Company, *Creativity, Challenge, and Courage* (Nagoya, Japan: Toyota Motor Company, 1983).

6. Zager, "Managing Guaranteed Employment," p. 108.

7. Jill Casner-Lotto, "Retraining Displaced Workers Is Seen as Urgent Need," *World of Work Report*, January 1983, p.1.

8. W. J. Rowland, "Buick Employe Development Center," an unpublished paper commissioned by Work in America Institute, June 1983.

9. "Memorandum of Understanding on National Issues between AT&T and CWA," *Daily Labor Report*, August 22, 1983, pp. D1-16.

10. "Communications Workers Begin Testing Technical Skills for Computer Job Bank," *Daily Labor Report*, January 10, 1983, pp. A1-2.

11. a. Jocelyn F. Gutchess, *Employment Security in Action: Strategies That Work.* Pergamon Press/Work in America Institute Series (New York: Pergamon Press, 1985).

b. Beck, "One Company's Strategy at Human Resource Management," p. 23.

12. Zager, "Managing Guaranteed Employment," p. 112.

13. Fred K. Foulkes and Anne Whitman, "Full Employment, Product/Marketing Strategies and Other Considerations," an unpublished paper commissioned by Work in America Institute, April 1984.

14. Beck, "One Company's Strategy at Human Resource Management," p. 23.

15. Gutchess, *Employment Security in Action*.

16. Claire Kolmodin, "Employment Security at Control Data

Corporation," an unpublished paper commissioned by Work in America Institute, June 1983.

17. Carey W. English, "Unions' Latest Goal: A Job for Life," *U. S. News and World Report*, May 21, 1984, p. 76.

18. Eric N. Berg, "Shrinking a Staff, the Kodak Way," *The New York Times*, September 4, 1983, section 3, p. 1.

19. Robert S. Eckley, "Company Action to Stabilize Employment," *Harvard Business Review* 44 (July-August 1966): 54-55.

20. Foulkes and Whitman, "Full Employment, Product/Marketing Strategies."

21. Ibid.

22. Ibid.

23. William Serrin, "The Way That Works at Lincoln," *The New York Times*, January 15, 1984, section 3.

24. Foulkes and Whitman, "Full Employment, Product/Marketing Strategies."

25. Ibid.

5.
Responding to Temporary
Economic Declines

Temporary economic declines are seasonal, cyclical, or occasional, generally lasting no longer than six months (unless aggravated by a sustained general recession). They are not necessarily related to the state of the economy. Early on, the employer has to determine whether the decline *is* temporary, a decision which carries risk because actions flow from it. The employer must also estimate the probable depth or severity of the decline. For example, Lincoln Electric's rule of thumb is that business rarely rises or falls more than 6 percent from the normal trend line, whereas other firms may experience regular swings of 20 percent.

A commitment to employment security implies that, in reacting to a temporary decline, the employer will defer layoffs as long as possible. Even so, a layoff is defined as a reduction in force, with the expectation that those laid off will eventually be recalled. (By contrast, a dismissal signifies that there will be no recall.)

If the employer expects to need the same number of employees at the end of the decline as before, and expects the decline to last no more than about six months, then layoff and recall are probably more expensive, in strict bookkeeping terms, than retaining people on the payroll, due to increased unemployment insurance payments and the high cost of bumping (see chapter 2).

Employment security companies take four broad lines of action to deal with a temporary decline: (1) restrict hiring, (2) make an effort to sustain the work load of protected employees,

(3) reduce payroll costs to match the reduction of work load, and (4) invest in "human capital." Since these strategies are not mutually exclusive, all four may proceed simultaneously. Layoffs are always the very last resort.

RESTRICTION OF HIRING

The first response to a declining work load is to restrict hiring and take as much advantage of attrition as possible. As employees quit, retire, or die, the employer determines whether the vacancies they leave need to be filled now or later. If a departing employee takes with him or her skills essential to the continuing operation of the firm even during the decline, these skills must be replaced without delay. The employer tries to replace them from the reservoir of current protected employees on at least a temporary basis. Failing that, it is necessary to recruit from outside. If the lost skills do not have to be in place until the decline ends, the employer has more lead time.

The utility of restricting hiring, however, depends on having plans and authority ready in advance, on having anticipated the pattern of attrition, and on being ready to go into action before the force of the decline hits. It also requires tough, high-level rules that effectively restrict hiring.

SUSTAINING THE WORK LOAD

In order to sustain the work load of protected employees, employers may withdraw work from nonprotected employees, increase demand for the firm's products or services, and reassign protected employees to useful work that is currently less valuable than their normal work or unrelated to current production.

Withdrawing Work from the Nonprotected

Firms that employ external "buffers" do so specifically in order to be able, when necessary, to reassign that work into the hands of protected employees. Temporary employees are released as soon as their contracts expire. Subcontracted work is retrieved wherever possible. Even firms that have issued subcontracts without intending to use them as buffers may, in a slump, bring manageable work back in-house. Since large firms rely on vendors and subcontractors for a substantial part of their finished or semifinished products, there is scope for such action. However, advance planning is needed to recapture this work without side-effects.

Increasing Demand

Some employment security firms believe that it takes extraordinary foresight to make successful marketing changes in time to counter a temporary decline. So they confine themselves to long-term strategies for steady growth. Others react more flexibly, with simple but effective measures. Lincoln Electric considers the following "the most reliable first line of attack for producing a temporary sales boost":

☐ Introduction of new products in time to generate orders during the slump. The company continually develops and introduces new products . . . but the best time for bringing out certain items is when the cycle is down.

☐ Cutting prices of existing products.

☐ Cutting costs in order to support profit margins in the face of price cuts. When production activity is high, cost reduction takes second place to getting out the product. . . . In slack periods management brings (production) deficiencies vigorously to the attention of the workers, who respond . . . with sharply higher productivity.

☐ Expanding the welding machine reconstruction business. . . . This segment of the business increases when purchases of new machines fall off. [1]

A special advantage of introducing new products during a slump is that the manufacturer has time for working out the inevitable "bugs" in production. By contrast, the usual pattern of introducing them when business is good creates havoc because the plant is already running at a high level. (Another company, reports Fred Foulkes, professor of management policy at Boston University, stresses the reverse side of the policy: it avoids *withdrawing* old products from the market during slumps, so as not to aggravate the loss of work load.[2])

Another strategy is to intensify the sales effort, often with the help of employees transferred from work units whose work load is down. The CEO himself may take the lead: Fred Foulkes cites a case of one CEO who "went on a selling trip that created an immediate market for the extra product." In any event, whatever may happen to other departments, the staffing of the sales department is protected or augmented. For example:

☐ When Bank of America recently closed some of its smaller branches, it moved some of the tellers and other administrative support people into the area of telemarketing.[3]

☐ When IBM needs additional resources in marketing support, systems engineering, branch office administration, or customer engineering, it retrains interested employees for new careers in the field.[4]

☐ During the 1980-82 economic recession as well as during earlier recessions, Lincoln Electric transferred office and factory workers to sales or sales support positions. Lincoln Electric posted these opportunities as it would any other jobs, interviewed the applicants, selected 50 people, and then put them through a six-week training period in the sales department. These people generated about $10 million in new sales.[5]

☐ Unions, on occasion, have teamed up with employers to increase sales during a slump as, for example, among members of the Jamestown Area Labor-Management Committee.[6]

☐ Materials Research Corporation is reported to have used surplus scientists and engineers to call on customers and for other lower-priority projects.[7]

☐ "Instead of laying off workers, shortening the workweek or cutting pay during the [1974] recession, Kimberly-Clark Corporation used 75 production workers to sell the consumer goods they normally produced, such as Kleenex tissues, towels, and diapers. This use of production employees let the company blitz an area not covered by the usual sales routes. The production workers became aware of the need for high quality and different production practices to contribute to productivity. Many workers discovered a new talent and made permanent shifts to sales jobs. The company registered an additional $250,000 in sales."[8]

☐ "Toyo Kogyo, the company building the Mazda, used 2,500 office and factory workers as salesmen for 8 months. Sales increased 30 to 40 percent."[9]

These sales efforts are not always backed by advertising campaigns. Clearly, they should be, although the reflex action of most employers is to cut back on advertising during a slump. Smart advertising can soften the impact of economic forces.

Occasionally, an employment security firm with spare capacity may assume subcontracts to perform work for other firms which have an excess of work load. (The defense industry is replete with instances of major companies—for example, aircraft manufacturers—subcontracting for one another. In multidivisional firms, such as IBM and Prudential Insurance, a division with a shortage of work may accept work from overly busy divisions.

When an entire industry is in temporary decline, it may be expedient for an employment security firm to expand its market share, even at the sacrifice of profit margins, as Japanese employers do.

Lower-Priority Work

When a firm is busy, many useful tasks are deferred or omitted, either because timing is optional or because their value to the firm is less than that of the employees' regular jobs. In a slump, the perspective changes and managers may seize the opportunity to catch up on deferred, neglected, or cyclical projects by assigning the work to surplus employees. Several of these projects are described below.

Manufacture for Inventory. As J.F. Lincoln wrote, "The cost of such production will be less in slack times because of (the) continuous production schedule (which it makes possible) and the lower material costs which usually accompany such times."[10] Lincoln Electric produces, for stock, parts and subassemblies rather than finished goods, mainly because the plant contains limited space for storing completed machines, and the dispersed warehouses are designed for rapid turnover. Lincoln's words, written when interest rates and carrying costs were relatively low, may be less forceful today.

An employer's willingness to manufacture for inventory depends on:

☐ The costs of financing surplus production, stockpiling and maintaining inventory, and paying state inventory taxes.

☐ The severity of cash-flow problems.

☐ The saleability of inventory within a reasonable time and at a fair price.

Deferred Maintenance. When a plant or office is running at full capacity, preventive and corrective maintenance gets short shrift, sometimes with costly consequences. Managers refuse to give up equipment time unless absolutely necessary. They postpone maintenance until the machine is clearly at or beyond break-down point, and operations often have to stop while demand is at its height. Conversely, maintenance departments staff to meet day-to-day needs.

Slack periods offer a welcome opportunity to catch up, particularly if surplus employees are willing and able to help. Effectively managed firms have plans at the ready, waiting for downtime. Workers are trained, flexible, and prepared.

Cross-training is particularly valuable for these occasions. A growing number of firms, especially those which organize semi-autonomous teams, train workers to carry out minor, or first-echelon, maintenance on the machines they operate. Employ-

---

How to Manage Employment Security: Temporary Declines

When companies experience a *temporary decline*, they can avoid layoffs by:

Restricting hiring

☐

Intensifying marketing efforts

☐

Assigning employees lower-priority
tasks, such as

manufacturing for inventory

maintenance

helping dealers

acting as consultants

☐

Training employees for flexible assignments

ment security also facilitates the cross-training of skilled maintenance workers, with remarkable gains in productivity and quality of work.

Paraconsultancy. During downturns, a number of Japanese companies assign their *best* workers to serve as paraconsultants. These workers are given time, access to tools, professional help, opportunity for outside training if they desire, and a free run of the plant, all with the aim of developing productivity improvements.

In the United States, the contract between Allied Tube and Conduit of Harvey, Illinois, and United Steelworkers Local 6939 provided for the assignment of "problem-solving tasks or training sessions" during periods of slack demand, instead of layoffs or short schedules. In September 1981, the parties agreed on a four-day workweek but then realized that, even so, there would be a surplus of 20 workers. The employer offered the latter a choice between layoff and the opportunity to be trained full time in problem solving, at full pay. Fifteen of the workers joined the program, which worked so well that the firm decided to extend the offer to every employee who wanted it.[11]

It is also worth noting that many American firms kept their quality circles and employee involvement teams going all through the 1980-82 recession.

Helping Dealers. Some Japanese companies lend surplus workers to their dealers (with whom they have a closer connection than most American companies) to serve as sales and/or repair people. A double benefit is realized: the dealers gain insight from the people who build the product; the workers gain insight from dealers' and customers' reactions to the product. Despite the different relationship that prevails here, a similar practice might be useful during downturns.

Lending Surplus Employees to External Organizations. This is an intriguing but thorny alternative. Difficulties do not arise when small groups of employees are lent without charge to civic or charitable organizations (for example, Kawasaki employees to the City of Lincoln, Nebraska; Prudential Insurance employees to various charities). But reimbursed loans to other private firms, particularly when large numbers of people are involved, appear to have created serious union problems for the receiving firms. In addition, wage sharing between lender and user should be included.

Most of the recorded cases have been in Japan (Kawasaki Steel/Isuzu Motors, Mitsubishi Heavy Industries/other Mitsubishi units, Sumitomo Metal Industries/other Sumitomo units, and Kawasaki Steel/Suzuki); in Germany (Weser/Daimler Benz); and in Luxembourg (Arbed/other companies). In the United States, the method has been used by a small electronics firm, the Verbatim Corporation, and by Lincoln National Life Insurance.[12]

It may be that a more structured, area-wide arrangement, based on an area labor-management committee, would make such exchanges more feasible. Analagous, although intracompany, area-hire plans have been in place for more than a decade among General Motors/UAW plants located in the same region.

RECOMMENDATION 12

As soon as employers detect the approach of a temporary decline in demand for their products or services, they should update and set in motion plans for (1) restricting hiring, (2) retrieving from temporary employees or subcontractors any work that can reasonably be done in-house, (3) expanding the demand for output, and (4) assigning surplus employees to lower-priority work.

REDUCING PAYROLL COSTS

When a firm's work load declines, the total number of work hours it requires usually declines roughly in parallel. The employer's key objective, however, is not to reduce work hours but to keep unit costs from rising because of surplus employees. The company may, therefore, try to reduce total employment costs at the same time that the work load is declining (although one shouldn't lose sight of the fact that in many cases the labor component is only a fraction of unit costs). This may be done by reducing wage and salary rates or benefits, or by reducing the number of hours worked.

When employees are asked to accept reduced earnings, whether there are quid pro quos or not, they demand equality of sacrifice. More and more employers now recognize the validity of this demand. Thus, there were extensive layoffs of white-collar as well as blue-collar workers in the 1980-82 recession (aside from the fact that white collars now outnumber blue collars in some industries). By the same token, workers and unions in some companies felt betrayed when executives received bonuses after workers had given concessions and many still remained on layoff.

Wage-Rate Reductions

In the 1980-82 recession, significant reductions of real hourly wage rates went into effect in many firms, nonunion as well as union. In some cases, the reductions were unilaterally imposed. In others, such as the auto industry, valuable trade-offs were negotiated: profit sharing, training and retraining, and greater employment security through lifetime employment experiments, the Guaranteed Income Stream Program, Mutual Growth Forums, and other arrangements. In the public mind these two disparate types of cases were lumped together as "concessions." The fact is that the great mass of both union and nonunion workers behaved with admirable restraint—and enlightened self-interest—throughout this difficult time.

Delta Air Lines furnishes an enviable example of mutual commitment. The company held off on wage cuts until the recession reached its depth, but at last had to give in. When it did, wages and salaries were reduced from top to bottom. The employees, to show their appreciation, pooled their savings and bought Delta a new Boeing 767.[13]

Intel accomplished much the same end, indirectly, by increasing the number of working hours per week without increasing earnings.[14]

Work Sharing

Work sharing is the practice of averting layoffs by reducing the number of hours of work, and wages in proportion, for the entire work force or an occupational segment of a company, rather than compelling part of the work force to bear the entire burden. For example, if a decline of work load makes 20 percent of the work force temporarily surplus, the most vulnerable 20 percent are *not* laid off; instead, the entire work force agrees to give up one day's work (that is, 20 percent of a five-day week) and one day's pay each week.

Unilateral reductions of work and pay as an alternative to layoffs are frequently imposed by nonunion employers, but these arrangements are not really considered work sharing. Properly, the term "work sharing" should be applied only where both employer and employees agree on a reduction.

Sharing the available work can take many forms, depending on the nature of the organization and its productive processes. The most common is reduction of the number of workdays per week, usually from five days to four. Other options include reducing the hours of work per day, shutting down the entire plant for a week or more, and alternating or rotating layoffs. In the latter arrangement, part of the work force is laid off for a period, after which it returns to work and another group is laid off for a similar period.

Union Contracts for Reduced Work Hours. Where there is a union, the subject of work sharing or layoff is a mandatory subject for collective bargaining. Since the 1975-76 recession, a new section heading for "work sharing, to avoid layoff" has been added to the index of the Bureau of National Affairs' *Labor Arbitration Reports*, indicating increased use of this technique.

Collective bargaining provisions that require or permit various kinds of work sharing are spread across a wide variety of manufacturing and nonmanufacturing industries. While some contracts call for mandatory division of available work, generally the use of work sharing is permissive. About one-third of the major contracts surveyed by the Bureau of Labor Statistics contain permissive clauses allowing reduction in hours, often up to one day a week, in place of layoffs. However, in only a few industries is work sharing systematically practiced.

Division-of-work clauses predominate in the apparel industry as a means of handling the variation in work loads that has always been part of the industry's operation. Procedures are generally worked out at the local level by the union representative and the employer. In some cases, work sharing takes the form of a shorter workweek for all employees. In other cases, where the reduction in work load is more serious, work sharing can take the form of alternate weeks of employment for the regular employees. In particularly difficult circumstances, layoffs do occur.

Reduction-in-hour clauses are found in many of the Bell Telephone System agreements with the Communications Workers of America and the International Brotherhood of Electrical Workers. In the steel industry, contracts with the Steelworkers provide local options to reduce work to 32 hours a week. Many construction industry unions, as well as the Graphic Arts and Teamsters unions, have also utilized forms of work sharing.

In 1974, the American Newspaper Guild signed an agreement with the *Washington Star* for a four-day week with a 20 percent reduction in salary as an alternative to layoff.

Although the principle is widespread, unions seldom invoke contractual rights to share work. Since the introduction of un-employment insurance, companies and unions are more likely to rely on seniority-based layoffs as a means of reducing the work force because (1) they know that lower-seniority workers who are laid off will receive enough in unemployment insurance bene-fits to survive on, and (2) unemployment insurance laws and regulations are biased against partial layoffs.

Unemployment Insurance Laws vs. Work Sharing. Under the current system, an organization whose production schedule re-quires it to reduce labor hours by 20 percent has, in theory, two options. It can lay off 20 percent of the work force, while the remaining 80 percent continue working full time and the 20 per-cent laid off become eligible for unemployment compensation. Alternatively, the organization can reduce everyone's work hours and pay by 20 percent. Should it do so by having them work four eight-hour days a week and take the fifth day off, unemployment compensation would probably not be paid for that fifth day. Although most states allow partial benefits for days lost in this manner, the formulas for computing benefits are so stringent as to be useless for work sharing, except in California, Arizona, Oregon, Florida, Illinois, Washington, and Maryland.

Generally, the benefit payable for part-week unemployment is reckoned as the benefit for a full week of unemployment minus wages earned during the week. Anyone whose earnings exceed the weekly maximum benefit is thus ineligible for benefits, even if unemployed for most of the week.

The basic federal-state unemployment insurance system is fi-nanced by employers through a payroll tax—called an "experi-ence-rated" tax because it is based in part on the employer's lay-off record. Extensive layoffs increase the employer's tax rate un-less the maximum has already been reached. Thus, some em-ployers, exploiting the provisions of the law that make employ-ees ineligible for partial benefits, schedule enough work each week so that employees earn just over the unemployment insur-ance limit and *then* lay them off for the rest of the week.

Employees in these situations are barred from collecting compensation, and the employer's experience-rated payroll tax is held down.

Some states raise additional legal impediments, such as waiting periods that make less-than-full-week unemployment impracticable. Where work sharing is used consistently, whether in union or nonunion shops, unemployment schedules may be keyed into local compensation requirements. For example, to avoid waiting-period requirements and maximum weekly pay limits, employees might work alternate weeks, thus becoming eligible to collect for their downtime.

In some states it may, nevertheless, be possible to obtain partial unemployment insurance benefits by means of layoff rotation. For example, in 1975, the Tomkins-Johnson Company, with plants in Michigan, Oregon, and Alabama, responded to the deep recession by putting 160 blue-collar (nonunion) employees on a rotation plan. For a period of four months, each employee worked four weeks and was laid off for the fifth week. This reduced each individual's work time by 20 percent, just as a four-day workweek would have done. The state paid full unemployment benefits for every fifth week.

The scheme was feasible because two of the states had no waiting period for benefits and one had a one-week waiting period, and because only the most junior production, maintenance, and technical employees—those whose base wages averaged only $30-$35 more than the maximum weekly unemployment benefit for which they were eligible—were rotated. Yet, had they claimed benefits for one day's layoff per week, they would have received nothing at all.

Reactions to the program, tested by means of attitude surveys, were highly favorable—so favorable that when it became necessary to reduce work time for secretarial, engineering, and customer-service employees in the 1980 slowdown, the same plan was put into effect.[15]

In the spring of 1980, "management and union representatives at the McCreary Tire & Rubber Company of Indiana, Pennsylvania, devised a furlough plan whereby each week one-third of the workers would be laid off on a rotating basis. During a four-month period, each group of employees worked and was paid for two out of three weeks. During the third week, the group was 'laid off' and collected unemployment benefits for that week. Employees also continued to be eligible for all fringe benefits.

"Although employees worked nine weeks less in 1980 than in 1979, because of vacation benefits, wage increases, and COLAs previously scheduled for 1980 in the union contract, earnings were within 1 percent of those in 1979. With unemployment benefits added, income levels were much higher.

"Reactions to the program were so favorable that when, toward the end of the four-month trial period, it appeared that an extension might be necessary, union members unanimously approved the plan. Since it would avoid the costly problems of recruiting and training new workers to replace those on furlough who would not return to work when recalled, management was also willing. During the furlough period, productivity improved, absenteeism decreased, the number of injuries dropped dramatically, and the percentage of scrap generated declined."[16]

☐ In 1982, Pan Am and the Teamsters agreed on three variants of work sharing, in one of which workers alternated 40-hour weeks, one week on and one week off.[17]

☐ In December 1983, when American Motors Corporation announced plans to lay off 700 hourly workers, UAW Local 72, in Kenosha, Wisconsin, recommended instead that the entire plant shut down for one week every five or six weeks.[18]

☐ At a nonunion employment security firm in 1974, management visited all the employees, plant by plant, and told people about the economic difficulties the company faced. All merit increases had been frozen; all exempt staff had taken 12 percent pay cuts. Management offered a choice: a layoff for 25 percent of the work force, or several weeks off without pay for everyone. Group meetings were held at every location. The employees chose the weeks off without pay.[19]

Other approaches to work sharing allow individual employees a range of choices. Given enough ingenuity, management and labor can develop schedules to meet the most diverse operating requirements and personal needs. For example, as an alternative to layoffs, United Airlines has combined job sharing with work sharing in a way that other companies and industries could replicate.

In the 1980 recession, United announced that it had to lay off 200 flight attendants. The Association of Flight Attendants agreed that economic conditions warranted belt tightening, but it rejected management's proposal. It made a counteroffer of a program for voluntary job sharing, which the company accepted.

Under the program, called "partnership time off," attendants volunteered to form job-sharing teams. In most cases, so that workers would share the burden of reduced hours, the teams consisted of one junior and one senior employee. The job sharers promised in writing that they would cover all assignments properly and work out by themselves the details of pay, benefits, and hours of work.

During the four-month program, United averted 125 out of 200 proposed layoffs. Flight attendants shared their jobs by alternating months or by determining who would fly on a trip-by-trip basis. Management found that the partnership-time-off program produced a more even geographical distribution of cutbacks, retention of trained flight attendants, and a reduction in absenteeism. The installation of this program also demonstrated the company's concern for its employees. Because of labor cutbacks, United extended the program for another five months.

At the end, 508 flight attendants were sharing jobs, and 365 jobs were kept on the payroll. In addition, because of the flight attendants' success story, the job-sharing concept spread to other company units, such as ticket agents.[20]

In Santa Clara County, California, county employees can take advantage of a variety of alternative work options—all of which are encouraged by collective bargaining agreements. Their choices include: job sharing, permanent part-time employment, flexible and compressed work schedules, and an unusual work-leisure trade-off arrangement called Voluntary Reduced Work Hours (VRWH). Although national AFL-CIO officials have opposed several of these options, the local unions of the Service Employees International Union have favored and, in some cases, originated these initiatives to offer workers a maximum number of options. Local union leaders felt that contract guarantees eliminated any dangers these new work options could pose to the unions' interests.

Under the contract agreement, for six months at a time, each employee may request a reduction of work time and pay of either 2.5 percent, 5 percent, 10 percent, or 20 percent. Each employee may take the time reduction either in the form of fewer hours per day or days per week or in longer blocks of time away from work. Employee and supervisor must agree on the arrangements. Although rules concerning overtime pay have been relaxed, the arrangements must produce no compulsory overtime or speed-ups for those who choose not to participate. Reductions do not affect fringe benefits, except for retirement contributions, which are tied to earnings.[21]

In a voluntary program at a nonunion company, where women make up a large part of the work force, employees have the option of taking a two- to four-week unpaid leave of absence during slack periods. Many women volunteer because they use the time to catch up with work at home.[22] A similar program of voluntary leaves of absence was carried out in 1980 by New York State's Department of Taxation, with AFSCME.[23]

In 1978 the State of California initiated a new approach to work sharing by enacting a law (based on West German experience) specifically adapted to the payment of partial unemployment insurance benefits, or short-time compensation (STC). Since then the states of Arizona, Oregon, Florida, Illinois, Washington, and Maryland have followed suit. Ironically, the State of New York, which initiated the U.S. campaign for STC in 1975, has not yet passed such a law. Canada has adopted a statute more liberal than any in the United States, and it has gained wide usage.

Because STC is a legislative matter, it is discussed in chapter 8 rather than in this chapter. (For a detailed account of STC, see a 1984 Work in America Institute/Pergamon Press book, *Short-Time Compensation: A Formula for Work Sharing* by Ramelle MaCoy and Martin J. Morand.)

Whether or not STC is available, successful work-sharing practices have two key features in common: (1) they operate within a time limit, and (2) they are voluntary measures jointly determined by employer and employees. Involuntary and protracted work-sharing measures, such as forced leaves of absence in the public sector, have not succeeded.

If a temporary decline in demand makes it essential to cut payroll costs faster than restricted hiring alone can do, the company, its employees, and its unions should jointly work out arrangements for temporarily reducing either wage and salary rates  *or the number of paid working hours. All stakeholders in the firm should share equitably in the hardship.*

RECOMMENDATION 13

INVESTING IN HUMAN CAPITAL

Japanese and West German employers invest heavily in training because they expect employees to stay with the company for most of their working lives. Some American employment security firms—especially those in high tech—do the same. The majority of U.S. firms, however, provide a minimum of training, in the belief that turnover is so high as to make training a waste of money.

A period of diminished work load is ideal for training and development activities. Education, training, and retraining work best when employees can give undivided attention to learning for a definite block of time. The entire work force may be available part time, or part of the work force may be available full time.

An employer can increase the value of its temporarily surplus employees at a cost not much greater than the cost of layoff. Instead of laying people off, the employer can place them on training/education status, pay them a stipend equivalent to unemployment insurance benefits, and help them learn skills that will benefit the employer.

Since employers eventually pay (in taxes) whatever their employees draw in unemployment insurance benefits, the only added costs are (1) fringe benefits, and (2) direct costs of training or education. In return, employers will have workers who are better trained and more loyal than before, and ready to apply their new abilities as soon as they are called back to work. The employees gain, too: they avoid discontinuity of service, the annoyance of collecting unemployment insurance benefits, and the misery of being "on the street"; they have more to offer the employer later on; and they are no worse off financially than they would be on layoff.

Like other employment security strategies, this one requires thoughtful preplanning. A stipend reserve fund must be established, and a curriculum must be prepared in advance.

RECOMMENDATION 14

To employees faced with layoffs, the employer should offer the alternative of remaining on the payroll and being paid the equivalent of unemployment insurance benefits while taking part in training and education programs approved by the employer.

LAYOFFS

Ultimate resort to layoffs in a temporary decline cannot be ruled out. If all other strategies prove inadequate to meet a cash-flow emergency, and if senior employees refuse to accept reduced earnings (even if supplemented by STC), the employer may have no alternative.

Nevertheless, the employees to be laid off embody a capital investment. The employer will want to ensure that, upon recall, they return as committed to the firm's success as before. It is incumbent on the employer, therefore, to consult with the employees and unions and demonstrate that layoffs are the least objectionable course under the circumstances. If employees and unions have been involved previously in planning the firm's strategy for combating the decline in demand, they will be more inclined than otherwise to believe the employer's case.

Before instituting layoffs, the employer should make it clear to employees and unions that no better solution was available.

RECOMMENDATION 15

NOTES

1. Robert Zager, "Managing Guaranteed Employment," *Harvard Business Review* 56 (May-June 1978): 110.

2. Fred K. Foulkes and Anne Whitman, "Full Employment, Product/Marketing Strategies and Other Considerations," an unpublished paper commissioned by Work in America Institute, April 1984.

3. Ibid.

4. Ibid.

5. Ibid.

6. Remarks by Robert W. Keidel at a meeting of the National Advisory Committee for "Employment Security in a Free Economy," a Work in America Institute policy study, June 15, 1983.

7. Stan Luxenberg, "Lifetime Employment, U.S. Style," *The New York Times*, April 17, 1983, section 3.

8. E. Bruce Peters, "Job Security, Technical Innovation, and Productivity," *Personnel Journal*, January 1978, p. 35, citing an article in *Business Week*, June 9, 1975, pp. 22-26.

9. Ibid., p. 35.

10. Zager, "Managing Guaranteed Employment," p. 110.

11. Rose Darby, "QWL Training Sessions Keep Allied's Employees at Work." *World of Work Report*, July 1982, p. 51.

12. Robert W. Keidel, "Intercompany Loans of Surplus Employees: A Critical Perspective," an unpublished paper commissioned by Work in America Institute, May 1983.

13. a. "Delta Executives Accept Salary Cuts," *The New York Times*, August 12, 1983, section D.

    b. Foulkes and Whitman, "Full Employment, Product/Marketing Strategies."

14. "The 125 Percent Solution," *World of Work Report*, June 1982, p. 48.

15. Jerome M. Rosow and Robert Zager, *New Work Schedules for a Changing Society* (New York: Work in America Institute, 1981), p. 93.

16. Jerome M. Rosow and Robert Zager, "Punch Out the Time Clocks," *Harvard Business Review* 61 (March-April 1983): 10, based on an article entitled "Work Sharing: A Rotational Furlough Plan Saves Jobs at McCreary Tire," by Linda Roberts, *World of Work Report*, February 1982, p. 9+.

17. "Pan Am Reaches Pacts on Wage Concessions with Three More Unions," *The Wall Street Journal*, December 23, 1982.

18. "Job Security and Income Security," *Kenosha (Wis.) News*, January 8, 1984, editorial page.

19. Fred K. Foulkes, *Personnel Practices in Large Nonunion Companies* (Englewood Cliffs, N.J.: Prentice-Hall, 1980), p. 111.

20. Rosow and Zager, "Punch Out the Time Clocks," p. 10.

21. Ibid., pp. 10-11.

22. Foulkes, *Personnel Practices in Large Nonunion Companies*, p. 108.

23. Maureen McCarthy and Gail Rosenberg, *Work Sharing Case Studies* (Kalamazoo, Mich.: Upjohn Institute for Employment Research, 1981), pp. 197-200.

6.
Responding to Permanent Declines of Work Load

Technological obsolescence, marketing shifts, intensified competition—these and many other reasons cause a work site to suffer a permanent loss of work load ("permanent" meaning "as far into the future as one can see"). The decline may affect one section of a work site, an entire site, or a whole division of a multidivisional firm; and it may affect any of those either in whole or in part. In every case, the event can be foreseen long before it happens, and the employer's interest is best served by informing the unions and affected employees as soon as possible. Thus, joint planning and countermeasures can be taken to anticipate and soften the adverse effects. Careful communication of plans and actions at every stage is vital.

The first response is an effort to replace the lost work load by tapping new sources. Should that fail, the employer may have to find ways to reduce the work force without dismissing people. If dismissals become unavoidable, the employer can at least ensure that displaced people are helped to obtain suitable jobs elsewhere. We are persuaded that outplacement assistance, in particular, has the potential to become a reliable backup for employment security in a free economy.

Employers intent on honoring a commitment to employment security should not be deterred by the permanent decline of demand for part or all of their output. In cooperation with their employees and unions, they should make every ef-

RECOMMENDATION 16

fort to replace the lost work load, reduce costs without dismissals and, if all else fails, help dismissed employees find suitable work elsewhere.

DEVELOPING ADDITIONAL WORK LOAD FOR PROTECTED EMPLOYEES

The permanent loss of work load from one's previous customers does not rule out the possibility of finding profitable work to do for other customers, although work sites controlled from organizationally distant headquarters often act as if it did. An employer committed to employment security will try various alternatives before giving up.

Buffers. As in the case of temporary declines, the employer will quickly bring back in-house any work currently being performed by temporary employees, subcontractors, or vendors.

New Products and Services. The employer can develop and introduce new products and services. Even companies that consider it impractical to launch new products during a temporary decline can move aggressively to counter a permanent loss of demand. As we have noted, the probability of loss always becomes clearly visible many months in advance; it is never a surprise, except to those who avert their eyes.

Subsidiaries. The employer may find it advantageous to introduce new products and services by acquiring or creating subsidiaries with greater latitude for innovation, and then transfer surplus employees to them. Japanese trading companies often take this route. Some U.S. companies, whose products have relatively short demand cycles, pursue the same goal by setting up the equivalent of internal subsidiaries. The 3M Company is one such employer.

Companies in high-tech industries plow large sums into research and development precisely in order to generate a continuing stream of new or improved products, because they know their competitors will get the jump on them if they don't. It is the intense competition and the investment in R&D that define an industry as "high tech," and not the other way around.

Subcontracts for Others. If a rival company does get the jump with a new product, and demand grows faster than the capacity to produce it, the company may be able to offset some of its own lost demand by obtaining a subcontract from the rival firm.

*In its efforts to offset perman-
ently lost demand, the employer
should, after retrieving from temporary employees and subcontractors work that can be done in-house,
consider launching new products or
services, acquiring or creating subsidiaries, or accepting subcontracts from other firms.*

REDUCING WAGE COSTS WITHOUT DISMISSALS

When a work site suffers a permanent loss of work load but
does not have to shut down, the employer who seeks to avoid
dismissals can (1) reduce the number of full-time-equivalent protected employees, (2) reduce unit-labor costs.

Reducing Numbers

Restricted Hiring. As in the case of temporary declines, the
employer should immediately restrict hiring and let attrition
bring down the number of protected employees. The corollary is
that surplus employees must be willing to fill the vacancies that
occur. Bank of America has been challenging the unemployment
insurance claims of those who turn down the offer of another
job with pay equivalent to that of their last job.

Work Sharing and STC. If attrition and restricted hiring cannot
accomplish the reduction in a reasonable time, the employer (and
union) should consider work sharing and STC (see chapters 5 and
8) as cost-reducing measures during the transition. If the majority
agree to work share, any protected employee who prefers not to
participate should be entitled to outplacement assistance.

Individualized Work Sharing. In place of work sharing across
the board, some employees may prefer to work part time for the
transition period, or even permanently. Some may choose job
sharing or voluntary reduced work hours (VRWH). The employer
should offer those individuals pro rata pay and benefits, with
suitable allowances for any adverse effect on pension rights.
Others may prefer unpaid vacations or leaves of absence.

A Louis Harris survey of the U.S. work force in 1978 reported
that between 30 and 40 million workers said they would trade
part of their current income for equivalent free time, particularly
if the free time could be enjoyed in larger blocks. The Bureau of

Labor Statistics also indicates a growing interest in longer vacations in lieu of higher salaries. In spite of the increased growth in paid vacations between 1968 and 1979, those favoring an additional full week of vacation *without pay* rose from 14 percent to 20 percent for men, and from 34 percent to 39 percent for women.[1]

Early Retirement. Early-retirement programs have reemerged as a major response to readjusting the size of the work force without resorting to forced layoffs.[2] They have marked advantages but also incur potential penalties in the long run.

Early-retirement programs are acceptable to management because they provide a stream of income to the separated employee and thus are much more palatable than forced layoffs. Another advantage is the fact that they are prefunded from pension-fund sources and only require a one-time added cost—an expense that can be rationalized easily in light of the projected longer-term multiyear payroll savings.

However, there are also disadvantages: (1) early retirement is heavily dependent upon the use of age as the primary criterion, and (2) these programs are fundamentally a negative, long-term response to the human condition, reflecting our economy's failure to provide full employment.

Trends. Early retirement is becoming an increasingly interesting option for both companies and employees.

☐ Last year, 17.4 percent of men over 65 were in the civilian labor force, compared with 22.8 percent in 1973 and 46.8 percent in 1948. The ratio of men between 55 and 64 who were still working also continued to drop, to 69.4 percent in 1983 from 78.3 percent in 1973 and 89.5 percent in 1948.[3]

☐ Of 305 companies responding to a survey by Hewitt Associates, 28 percent said they had offered early-retirement programs between 1980 and 1982. State governments and colleges also are dangling incentives before their senior employees. In Ohio, for example, some 70 state colleges and public school districts are crediting early retirees with as many as five additional years of service to fatten their pensions. Although new early-retirement programs have diminished in number as the economic recovery has gathered steam, a number of big companies are still offering them.[4]

☐ During the recession, retirement incentive programs were promoted widely by such companies as Bethlehem Steel, Deere & Company, Exxon, Firestone Tire & Rubber, AT&T, Sears

Roebuck, Bank of America, Eastman Kodak, the Sun Company, and many others on the Fortune 500 list.[5]

Advantages of Early Retirement. Early-retirement programs are almost ready-made solutions to serious overstaffing in any major organization with a well-funded pension plan, an older work force, and sufficient cash flow to budget the one-time incentive costs.

Such programs reduce the pressure to lay off or separate younger workers or those in mid-career who are projected to have many more years of potential service than the early-retirement target group. Therefore, these programs tend to be more popular with younger, middle and upper-level managers who see the program as their opportunity for recognition and advancement. At the same time, the company is making a conscious de-

---

How to Manage Employment Security: Permanent Declines

When companies experience a *permanent decline,* they can avoid dismissals by

Making an effort to replace lost demand by
developing new products
establishing subsidiaries
subcontracting for other companies

☐

Reducing costs without dismissals by
restricting hiring
work sharing
early retirement
phased retirement
productivity programs

cision to dismiss older career professional, managerial, and executive personnel in order to retain younger people. Not only are the per capita costs of younger employees lower, but they comprise the next generation of management.

Early-retirement programs are also viewed as socially responsible, on balance, and so do not create adverse public relations. Exceptions to this will occur in so-called "company towns," where one major employer virtually dominates the labor market and where the programs, even though voluntary, tend to represent a threat to the entire community.

The strongest virtues of the early-retirement technique are that it provides strong financial incentives for leaving and permits self-selection on the part of employees. Since the employees who elect to leave volunteer for a variety of reasons, and since the entire program is seen as a response to external economic circumstances, management can feel free of guilt. Of course, some of the employees who do not make informed choices may regret their decision or seek to reconsider their action, but this adverse side-effect can be minimized by providing a longer "open-window" period for decision making and by offering a preretirement counseling program.

One of the financial advantages of this approach to the rebalancing of the work force is the ease with which it can be financed in large organizations. Most of the financing is available through previously funded pensions already written off as personnel expense in prior years. Therefore, the funds do not impose any strain on operating costs. The special one-time cost can be substantial, but it is written off in one year and distributed across the corporation rather than charged to individual divisions or departments. Thus, the costs are attributed to the organization as a whole, but the short-term savings and reduced projected expense are credited to the individual operating department. When managers reduce their personnel costs in this relatively painless way, with no change in their operating budgets, the financial picture looks excellent in the short term, and managers look and feel better.

Further, early-retirement programs are easy to finance in today's economy because corporations have reduced the normal retirement age. Whereas 65 or even 67 was the normal retirement age in the 1960s, many companies now use age 60 as the full-retirement age, and many organizations (such as government agencies) use age 55, with 30 years' service, as a full-retirement standard. Since the number of years remaining to retirement has been reduced, it has become less costly to extend early-retirement options to people in their mid- and even early 50s.

From the standpoint of the total work force, there are marked advantages to an early-retirement program versus layoffs and dismissals. From the perspective of the early-retirement target group, choice is critical, as is the opportunity to time the date of separation to take place under relatively honorable circumstances, to receive lifetime income, and to leave the organization for a life of leisure or part-time employment. Many postretirement studies have reported that a preponderance of adjustments to early retirement are favorable, especially after a few years have elapsed and individuals have had an opportunity to develop some perspective on the change.

Disadvantages of Early Retirement. There are serious disadvantages to early-retirement programs despite their popularity. Generally, the most serious weakness pertains to the fact that, although described as voluntary, early retirement is frequently a forced choice. (This is less likely to be true of blue-collar workers, who often welcome early retirement because their work is more physically demanding and less rewarding.) For the individual, an early-retirement program may mean a foreshortened career; for the organization, it represents a risky trade-off: the loss of large numbers of highly paid senior personnel from a cross-section of the organization, without any guarantee that ready replacements of equal skill and experience are available. The very fact that an early-retirement program has been adopted is evidence that the organization did not have a long-term, human-resource strategy.

Although large organizations that are well financed can afford to offer generous incentives, these programs are not cheap. For example, Sears, Roebuck and Company made reductions in its executive ranks in 1980, but the retirement offer cost the company $66.7 million to put into effect. A major plan offered by Kodak last year resulted in an after-tax charge of $87.4 million against first-quarter earnings. New York State estimates the bill for its special early-retirement program at $145 million, spread over five years, and cautions that if many of the 8,000 jobs vacated last year are refilled, the state stands to lose money on the program. Therefore, the cost factor needs to be subjected to more careful cost-benefit analysis, and the organization needs to consider other alternatives, especially when the program is truly voluntary and the company risks losing a segment of high-talent management. In fact, short-term savings should be subjected to a five-year carry-forward analysis, taking into account the rate of replacement, in order to determine the actual savings in the long term.

One of the serious problems created by early-retirement plans is that the voluntary element is not always entirely genuine. Employees caught in the early-retirement squeeze may be offered unattractive alternatives, such as transfer, demotion, reassignment, or career stalemate if they reject the incentive program. There are two forces at work compelling the older worker to move out: One is the carrot of financial incentives and the other is the stick of punishment for resisting in situations of implied duress. These stories tend to circulate in the community, and inside the company, with adverse effects on both employee morale and public opinion.

The company is caught on the horns of a dilemma in deciding whether to be entirely honest in its approach to these programs or to modify the element of chance by imposing criteria, generally based on performance, potential, and organizational need.

This decision poses a serious problem for the company, since experience has shown that the best performers are the most confident and the most likely to make a smooth transition to another company at equal or better pay and opportunity. By encouraging early retirement, the company deprives itself of these talents and may inadvertently push the employee into the open arms of competitors. On the other side of the coin, if the company does not extend an equal retirement opportunity to the most capable employees, it may be seen as discriminating against members of the organization who are less efficient, less satisfactory performers, and less deserving of special incentives. Those who have adhered to completely voluntary programs have incurred serious hidden losses, rarely measured and often too painful to quantify, as a result of this dilemma.

Among the indirect effects of early-retirement programs is the psychic shock to the organization. Essentially, these programs run counter to demographic trends in our society and the growing interest in extension-of-work-life programs. They also ignore the fact that the number of young people entering the work force each year is rapidly declining, resulting in a concentration of people in the middle years.

The Amendment to the Age Discrimination in Employment Act to extend working life to age 70 and the recent move to eliminate the age ceiling must be contrasted with early-retirement programs that terminate careers of people in their early 50s. These programs would seem to reveal an outmoded belief by many companies that older workers are less productive and less motivated than other workers and thus more expendable. It also ignores the fact that men and women in their mid-50s have at least 15 productive years of work ahead. The disposal of these most experienced, loyal, and talented members of the work force represents a waste of human resources, since many who would like to resume full-time employment after retirement are unable to relocate in similar careers because of age discrimination. Thus, for the nation as a whole, the macro effect of hundreds of early-retirement programs is contrary to the requirements for economic growth.

Moreover, an early-retirement program that cuts a wide swath across the organization affects the remaining employees adversely. All employees, but especially those who are a few years away from early-retirement age, feel insecure about their future. They realize that dedicated, loyal employees, who are committed to a lifetime in the company, can never again feel certain as to when or how their careers will be aborted.

When early-retirement programs occur two or three times in succession, they deliver a clear message that investment in the future is highly questionable and that dedication, high productivity, and loyalty to the firm will not necessarily result in a full career and retirement at the age set forth in the company's pension plan, or even several years later, as now provided in the law of the land.

Consequently, in attempting to balance the pros and cons of early-retirement programs, top management should look at all of the options; it certainly should resist the temptation of rushing into early-retirement programs at the last minute, when production, profits, and economic conditions look the worst.

To the extent that these programs represent an emergency short-term adjustment to unload costs, they may fail to fulfill the long-term needs and objectives of corporate growth and competitiveness. To the extent that the people who leave are a fair cross-section of the total work force and that their departure is a necessary feature of forward-looking strategy for the next five to ten years, these programs offer a more responsible and socially acceptable answer to change. And if the surgery is clean, relatively painless, and not frequently repeated, it may represent the most valid choice under the circumstance. Although preferable to dismissal, early retirement is a mixed blessing, popular with the younger up-and-coming group but worrisome to older workers who do not feel ready to retire.

Phased retirement. A promising alternative to early retirement is early *semi*retirement, or phased retirement. This strategy has been tried by at least one private-sector firm (Deere & Company) and has been widely used in California school systems. In 1982 some 965 teachers in 150 school districts of that state participated in the Reduced Workload Program, which gave teachers aged 55 or over the opportunity to work half time, at half-time pay, while continuing to receive full benefits and full service credit toward retirement. More than 100 of those working half time shared jobs with other teachers.[6]

In a pilot survey of 266 older employees of Lockheed/California and of the City of Los Angeles, half of the interviewees indicated interest in extending their working lives by means of part-time work, flexitime, job modification, or job transfer (part time was the most preferred), provided they were not forced to take a cut in base pay or forgo drawing at least part of their pension. Most of those favoring part-time work wanted to work fewer days per week rather than fewer hours per day.[7]

In Sweden, older workers between the ages of 60 and 65 may opt to share their current jobs with another worker, reducing by at least five hours a week the average workweek (the minimum workweek is 17 hours on average). Those who participate in this plan are entitled to claim a special partial pension, which is set at 65 percent of the difference between their income while working full time and working part time. At age 65, if they continue to work part time, they are no longer eligible for the partial pension, but may receive half of the normal pension.

A survey by Sweden's National Social Insurance Board reveals that, as of April 1978, about 25 percent of all eligible employees aged 60 to 65 had enrolled in the plan. The board estimates that the reduction of total working hours by 50 percent will result in only a 13.8 percent loss of income for job sharers.[8]

REDUCING UNIT LABOR COSTS

If the survival of the work site requires that unit labor costs be held at a reduced level even after the number of protected employees has been brought down permanently, the employer (and union) may have to negotiate pay and benefit reductions and/or sharply accelerate the rate of productivity increase. Over the years, unions have accepted such bitter pills when persuaded that they were genuinely necessary. In return, they have negotiated for quid pro quos, such as stock transfers, profit sharing, representation on the board of directors, restrictions on plant closings, or an explicit commitment to future employment security.

Productivity improvement programs conducted under the threat of a plant closing or reduction in force have often saved employee jobs.

☐ General Motors' obsolescent assembly plant in Tarrytown, New York, was on the verge of closing when its noted QWL program was launched. Many dismissals were averted, although the 1980-82 recession took a heavy toll.[9]

☐ The Ford Motor Company's transmission plant at Sharonville, Ohio, was also in serious trouble until its Employe Involvement program helped make it a company leader in productivity and quality.[10]

☐ A small plant in Tuscaloosa, Alabama, which supplies General Motors with carburetors, escaped closure with the aid of a productivity program planned with the engineering school of the University of Alabama, at Tuscaloosa.[11]

☐ Since 1982, three major airlines—PanAm, American, and Eastern—have staved off large-scale dismissals by means of a combination of wage cuts, employee share holding and board representation, work-rule changes, and joint productivity programs.[12]

However, unions seem no longer willing to accept reductions if they believe there is no hope of regaining the lost volume.

If it becomes necessary to reduce payroll costs permanently, the employer should first try to do so without dismissals, using such methods as restricted hiring, work sharing, early retirement, phased retirement, wage reductions, and intensive productivity-raising programs.

RECOMMENDATION 18

WHEN DISMISSAL IS UNAVOIDABLE

When, despite the employer's best efforts, dismissals cannot be avoided, there are still honorable ways to uphold the commitment to employment security: (1) the employer can help displaced employees obtain suitable new jobs, and (2) if the local labor market is inadequate, the employer can help replace the lost jobs.

Help with Reemployment

Bridging Assistance. Some of the dismissed employees will be able and willing to get new jobs on their own. A portion of those who have spent several years with one employer will find that the jobs most readily available to them offer starting pay and benefits below their current ones, although prospects for the future may be good. The employer can reduce this obstacle and broaden the range of opportunity by providing bridging assistance.

☐ The most useful assistance would be a commitment to make up, for a specified time period of three, six, nine, or twelve months, any shortfall of pay suffered by reason of taking the new job. This transition payment eases movement and increases outside employment options.

☐ As an alternative, the employer can offer a lump sum or monthly payment calculated to offset the expected shortfall.

Pension portability is another form of bridging assistance. The employer might arrange to have the employee's pension rights, whether vested or not, transferred to the new employer's plan. Although most employers oppose the principle of pension portability on the ground that the essential point of a pension is to cement loyalty between employee and firm, that argument loses its force when the employer itself asks an employee, who is not at fault, to leave.

Outplacement. Most displaced employees have marketable skills but lack the ability to find a job. Practically every displaced worker is a candidate for outplacement assistance. Outplacement for managers and professionals is growing in popularity and has proved its value. Outplacement assistance for rank-and-file employees is on the increase, but remains the exception rather than the rule.

Important social innovations sometimes have strange origins.

Outplacement began as a euphemism for easing less-effective executives out of one firm and into another. This was a face-saving strategy that reduced personal loss for the employee and diminished the employer's potential legal liability for discrimination. These origins should not obscure the potential of outplacement

---

How to Respond to
Unavoidable Dismissals

When dismissals are unavoidable, employers can help employees make the transition to a new job by means of

Cushioning the transition to lower-paying jobs

☐

Portability of pension rights

☐

Outplacement assistance

☐

Retraining for new jobs

☐

Training and counseling for self-employment

☐

Subcontracts for those who purchase
part of the company

☐

Sale of the company to employees

☐

Converting physical facilities for new businesses

☐

Incentives to new businesses

as a bridge to employment security, when all else fails. It can apply equally to individuals and large groups of employees at all levels in the organization. Indications are that outplacement for blue-collar employees is remarkably inexpensive—far less expensive than unemployment insurance or severance pay.

Practitioners of self-directed job search have achieved placement rates averaging 74 percent for a broad spectrum of displaced employees, at a cost of about $600 per employee assisted.[13]

In outplacement: (1) the employee exercises primary responsibility for obtaining the new job, and (2) the employer contributes counseling and support services. These programs vary in regard to how long the employer's help continues, the kinds of support services provided, the nature of training in job-search methods, the geographical range of job search, whether relocation help is included, whether skill training or retraining is provided, and whether outplacement begins before or after dismissal.

As long as the employer furnishes counseling and support until the employee actually lands a suitable job, outplacement can be shaped into an effective tool of employment security. It has been used to help blue-collar people at Corning Glass, Howard Johnson, and major rubber companies, among others.

For example, when Dana Corporation closed its Edgerton, Wisconsin, plant in 1980, 300 employees faced dismissal. Some 250 of them took part in an 18-hour job-search training course conducted by Dana staff. The course included preparation of a skills inventory, resume writing, improving communications skills, and financial and retirement planning. In cooperation with the United Auto Workers and the Wisconsin Job Service, the company set up a "job center" in the plant, with desks, reference materials, newspapers, bulletin boards for job notices and success stories, microfiche equipment, and free telephones. Employees worked on the buddy system, for mutual support. Dana managers mailed letters to 3,250 employers in the region with machine operations like their own, listing all the displaced employees and their skills. "The response was astounding, and the requests were tremendous. It proved again that only about 30 percent of available jobs are listed or advertised," said one of the managers. Of the 250 employees in the job-search program, "86 percent of the hourly and 95 percent of the salaried employees found jobs," although the deepening recession caused the search to take longer than usual and also caused some of the replacement jobs to be lost.[14]

Some companies have advertised their employees' availability through job fairs, newspaper articles, postings, and ads. For example, GTE held a job fair for surplus employees at a plant in Chicago. Many large firms in the area attended, and nearly all the surplus people were placed in one day. They received full severance benefits but needed no unemployment insurance.

Other companies that have used outplacement for blue-collar workers include Goodyear Tire and Rubber, Firestone Tire and Rubber, Sears Roebuck, Colonial Penn Group, Amoco Chemical, Celanese, Conoco, Monsanto, and Warner Lambert. For example:

☐ Goodyear expected to save $3 million of unemployment insurance by spending $300,000 on outplacement for 1,450 hourly employees.

☐ Amoco Chemical placed 80 percent of 225 hourly people displaced when the plant was destroyed by fire.

☐ Monsanto placed 65 percent of 1,400 hourly employees displaced when it withdrew from the polyester filament business.[15]

The fee for outplacing a manager ranges from 15 to 30 percent of annual compensation, and help is usually open-ended—continuing until a job is found. Counselors report that most of the people they assist do find jobs, and the large majority of jobs they find pay at least as well as the jobs they left. As a rule of thumb, it takes one month of job search for each $10,000 of salary.[16]

Job-search training rests on the discovery that most available jobs are not visible to the naked eye. The applicant has to flush them out with phone calls, resumes, cover letters, supporting references, carefully rehearsed interview techniques, and evaluation of job offers. That is, the applicant has to know and do all that an employment agency would do.

For most people, outplacement begins as a traumatic experience, although it often leads to a satisfying result. There are valid reasons for trauma: dismissal arouses a sense of failure and guilt, the employer has not previously mentioned the possibility of outplacement, and employees are frightened of the job market and unaware of the invisible market. With proper presentation and notice, these difficulties can be overcome.

The displaced employee finds it hard to concentrate on job search while faced with more immediate questions of how to keep family and possessions together. It is best, therefore, for outplacement to begin before dismissal. Transitional assistance might include: a "benefit umbrella" of health, disability, and life insurance; severance based on age plus grade plus service; tuition reimbursement for those who need a high school diploma; arrangements for help by community and government agencies; arrangements with local banks to avert foreclosures; availability of social workers; church- or community-furnished day care for children; coordination with the unemployment insurance system.

Retraining. Some employees are unskilled, or have skills for which there is no market in the area, but they have the capacity to acquire new skills. If outplacement fails, they need a program of training or retraining, followed by job-search training. The cost of retraining might be traded for the employee's accrued vacation rights.

The extent of the national need for retraining displaced employees is debated, even in such hard-hit industries as autos and steel; the answer will not be clear until suitable job vacancies appear in areas where the displaced are willing to work. To retrain people "on spec" would only make matters worse. Progressive firms are moving cautiously, matching their efforts to the real demands of the job market.

☐ A declared goal of the UAW-Ford Employe Development and Training Program, with respect to dismissed employees, is to build a "delivery network (of training programs) linking local managements, local unions, and community resources throughout the country where Ford facilities are located."[17] The goal is being met, according to Donald Ephlin, UAW vice-president and former director of the UAW-Ford division. (He presently serves in the same capacity for the UAW-GM division.)

Each Ford work site is encouraged to form a joint committee, with its own plans, and to use the services of the Dearborn Center. By January 1984, 4,200 dismissed employees had been retrained, or helped to gain vocational reeducation. Among the occupations chosen were microwave technician, computer repair and maintenance worker, video production worker, cable TV technician, licensed practical nurse, electrical engineering technician, robotics technician, auto body mechanic, computer numerical control machinist. A high rate of placements is claimed.[18]

☐ General Motors, the UAW, and the State of California in 1982 launched a $10 million pilot program to provide job counseling, retraining, and placement services for 8,400 dismissed California workers. By January 1983, 300-400 auto workers had completed vocational education and retraining classes. Job-development efforts were centered on industries known to be expanding in California: installation of smog-control devices in cars; prison construction; aerospace; high-tech industries.[19] (See chapter 7 for a description of outplacement and retraining programs by California's Plant Closure Response Unit, the California Employment Training Panel, and the Downriver Community Conference.)

The strongest motivator and morale builder for retraining is knowing that the curriculum is essential to a job that one is about to undertake. It follows that the best use of retraining money is probably to help displaced workers get new jobs and then pay the new employers to retrain them.

Retraining programs usually begin with an assessment of learning capacity which, with disturbing frequency, reveals sizable numbers of people who need remedial education.

Self-Employment. This may be the goal of some employees who have hobbies or skills that can be converted into a full-time business.

IBM's Retirement Education Assistance Plan, launched in 1977, provides potential retirees and their spouses with $2,500 each in tuition aid, starting three years before retirement eligibility and ending two years after retirement. The purpose of the plan is to help develop new interests and/or prepare for a second career. A wide variety of courses meet the intent of the program, including real estate, television and radio repair, interior decorating, creative writing, musical instruction, carpentry, photography, hotel management, and accounting.

In 1979, 1,200 people completed their courses of study, 50 percent more than in the previous year. While television, radio, and motor repair, as well as real estate, were the most popular areas, one IBM annuitant became a tennis pro, having used the plan to attend tennis college. Another took voice lessons and became a professional singer. Another opened his own picture-framing shop. One retiree became a gemologist after studying that specialty. Another planned to start a Chinese food catering business.[20] Similar programs are sponsored by the Swedish Employment Security Council (see chapter 7).

The employer should designate a staff person to advise would-be self-employers on the viability of their business plans, on location, and on similar questions. In addition, the employer should offer loans at favorable rates and use the interest payments to help finance subsequent self-employers.

The employer may have a continuing need for some of the services that individual displaced employees can provide. Often the employer engages an employee as a consultant, contracting for enough time to ensure the viability of self-employment until the employee can acquire other clients and become independent, as in the case of entrepreneurial subcontracts.

Entrepreneurial Subcontracts. Occasionally a change of process or of market demand makes the output of one department partially superfluous, and the displaced employees may offer to run it as an independent business, provided the company is willing to award them a long-term contract to supply its needs.

An article in *The Economist* in June 1983 described entrepreneurial subcontracting programs in Europe:

> Expensive, full-time workers are being turned into cheaper, independent subcontractors by a growing number of companies in Europe. Skilled white-collar workers can cost employers up to three times their basic salary in office space, fringe benefits and other overheads. By turfing them out and signing contracts for their services, companies can cut costs and still retain people they can trust. Employees are keener than they were to set up on their own. Widespread redundancies have made working for big firms seem less secure and those reemployed in this way like to think of themselves as "entrepreneurs."
>
> Rank Xerox, the British copier-maker, caused a splash last year when it sold computer terminals to about 20 employees and gave them contracts to work from their homes for the company for a maximum of 100 days a year. ICI, the British chemical giant, followed suit by seconding employees to their own businesses, and initially guaranteeing their income. Two of ICI's computer men . . . who did not want to move when their department was transferred elsewhere, founded their own computer firm. . . . ICI helped them to establish their business and subcontracted work to them. . . .
>
> Artes Graficas, a Spanish printing company, converted its entire photo-composition unit, employing 53 people, into a subcontractor last year. The unit, which was inefficient and caused mayhem in other parts of the company, was sold

to a group of managers and workers. It now has a full order book and is profitable.

At the opposite end of Europe, a Finnish paper company has sold its tree-harvesting machines to the machine operators. The company, Enso-Gutzeit, guaranteed its employees' bank loans, helped them to form their own firms and then offered them contracts to do their old jobs. Another Finnish company, Tammerneon, a maker of neon lights, has converted part of its plant into an independent business owned by former employees. They rent all the equipment they need from Tammerneon, and work on contracts.

Subcontracting has led to big gains in productivity for Tammerneon and most of the other companies that have experimented with it. The Finnish tree harvesters do about 30 percent more work than before because they are more careful with their machines, and do much of the maintenance in their own time. The Spanish photo-composition plant does now twice as much work as before for its former owner, Artes Graficas, using only 18 people: the rest of its workers are busy on contracts for other customers.

On Clydeside (U.K.), Mr. J.N. Naisby, former head of security at the UIE shipyard, reports a sharp drop in absenteeism since he became an independent subcontractor and brought most of the people working under him into a new company. Though they still do the same job in the same place, Mr. Naisby's dozen or so employees have between them missed work on only about 15 days in the past 2½ years: before the new company was formed, the 20 men then on the job went absent for a total of roughly 700 days a year. [21]

Help Replace the Lost Jobs

Outplacement and other aids to reemployment serve their purpose only to the extent that the labor market has suitable jobs available for the displaced. At certain times and places in the United States there may just not be enough jobs to go around, even after taking into account the fact that most vacancies are not visible. An employment security firm will act to replace the loss of jobs in the area by selling the business to its employees, by converting the physical facilities, or by attracting new employers in other ways. Such efforts involve cooperation with other employers, unions, and government bodies (see chapter 7), but an individual firm can take some initiatives alone.

Sale of the Business. When a work site is on the verge of closing and the local job market is desperate, the employees—perhaps with community backing—may offer to buy the business, usually through an ESOP. A conscientious employer may be tempted to sell, but will not agree until satisfied that the purchasers have a reasonable hope of making a go of it. Self-imposed wage cuts, dismissals, hard work, cooperation, and devoted, capable managers may not be enough to overcome plant obsolescence, shortage of working capital, or basic market shifts. A case in point is Rath Packing Company, which, after years of struggle as an employee-purchased company, asked for reorganization in mid-1984 under Chapter XI of the Bankruptcy Act and began negotiating for acquisition by an outside party.

In other instances, however, the outcome has been more fortunate, though often at the price of wage reductions, dismissals, and the investment of needed personal savings. Among the larger survivors are:

☐ Hyatt Clark Industries, Clark, New Jersey (ball bearings)
☐ Weirton Steel, Weirton, West Virginia
☐ Republic Hose Manufacturing Corporation, Youngstown, Ohio (high-pressure hose)
☐ Jamestown Metal Products, Jamestown, New York (metal furniture)
☐ Saratoga Knitting Mill, Saratoga Springs, New York (fabrics for women's apparel)
☐ Bates Fabrics, Lewistown, Maine (bedspreads).

It has been estimated that these six buyouts alone preserved more than 9,000 jobs in the plants themselves, in addition to several thousand more jobs among suppliers and local merchants.[22]

Buyouts are not limited to manufacturing plants. In the autumn of 1982, United Food and Commercial Workers Local 1357 arranged for its members to purchase two A&P supermarkets in Philadelphia which had been set for closing. The ex-employees organized as a worker-owner cooperative and re-opened the stores under the name of 0 & 0 (worker-owned and -operated). By mid-1983, the local was negotiating to buy two more stores.[23]

Conversion of Physical Facilities. If the employer owns the work site that is to be closed, it can make certain that the next use of the physical facilities provides the largest possible number of jobs. William Batt, quality of work life advisor to the Labor Department's Bureau of Cooperative Labor-Management Relations and Programs, has recorded several instructive cases:

☐ "In 1960, when Ford closed its old Chester, Pennsylvania, factory, it had two purchase offers. The higher bid was from Scott Paper, which wanted to use the plant for warehousing, and the other was from Reynolds Metal, which wanted to use it for manufacturing." At the state's request, "Ford agreed to offer Reynolds the opportunity to match the higher bid, which Reynolds promptly took."[24] The plant continued running until 1982.

☐ In the early 1960s, when General Electric closed a plant in Clyde, New York, it "donated the plant to a local development corporation set up for this purpose. GE also helped Clyde find a supplier located in Cleveland to purchase it. Clyde then used the proceeds from the sale to develop an industrial park on adjacent land and to bring in other employers. The Area Redevelopment Administration helped out with loans and grants for sewer and water lines. The town ended up with more jobs and more diversification than it had had before GE closed the plant."[25]

☐ In Europe: (1) the British Steel Corporation's subsidiary, BSC Industry, Ltd., rents space inexpensively to new firms in its old steel buildings, or in new plants specially constructed on old mill properties, and (2) Rhone-Poulenc, the French chemical manufacturer, follows a similar policy.[26]

Attracting Small Employers. The employer can use various means to induce other employers to begin or expand operations in the area. Some 20 to 25 French firms, seeking new jobs for redundant employees, have made special efforts to attract small employers. The range of inducements includes: cash for each job provided; loans or loan guarantees; subsidized interest rates; assistance in obtaining government subsidies; equity participation; the gift—or low-price sale—of land, buildings, and equipment; selection and training of personnel; technical or marketing-feasibility studies; search for joint-venture partners; guaranteed purchase of output; help in cutting red tape. Sometimes the help is contingent on hiring displaced employees; usually the only requirement is siting within a prescribed radius of the endangered workplace.

It is not usually very useful to solicit firms in a related industry, because their employment patterns are similar to those of the soliciting firm.

Strategies used by various companies to induce small employers to locate in the affected area are described below:

☐ Tate and Lyle, Britain's leading sugar refiner, had to close refineries in 1977-79. As a means of protecting the displaced employees, the company decided to invest between 10,000 and 20,000 pounds per job in existing viable enterprises that needed capital to expand and that agreed to give "first refusal" to ex-Tate and Lyle employees. Erskine Westayr, a small electrical engineering company with a growing market in household appliances but insufficient capital, agreed to locate in the affected area, bringing 150 jobs.

Tate and Lyle also created, with an investment of 14 million pounds, a wholly owned subsidiary, Talres Development, to develop and market biodegradable chemicals. BSC Industry does not provide direct financial assistance, but helps companies obtain such assistance from various sources. It also provides specialist services in market research, technical studies, and location analysis at no cost to the client company. Also BSC Industry provides low-cost space in refurbished steel-plant outbuildings for small businesses, and erects new buildings in cooperation with local development agencies. For example, a closed foundry near Glasgow attracted 54 small companies, with almost 400 employees, within four months of opening. (A similar BSC Industry workshop in Cardiff, Wales, has sheltered 73 new businesses, of which only 3 failed; 16 moved out to expand.[27]) Each company paid a commercial-rate rent but had the right to move out without penalty on three months' notice. Having a variety of businesses on the premises left the community less susceptible to the ups and downs of a single major employer.[28]

☐ The British American Tobacco Company (BAT) set aside a closed plant in Liverpool for use by dismissed employees who wanted to start their own businesses. BAT provided training, technical support, and other incentives.[29]

☐ In France: Thomson (electrical) has brought a textile firm, a maker of woodcutting machinery, a furniture maker, and a dairy firm into an area in which a plant reorganization has eliminated 700 jobs. Rhone-Poulenc (chemicals) encourages its ex-employees to exploit the company's little-used patents. BSN (food, glass) has helped chemical firms and a manufacturer of office furniture. Rhone-Poulenc has helped create over 2,000 jobs; St. Gobain (glass), hundreds of jobs. Other companies have saved the towns where their plants were located.[30]

On occasion, European firms take equity positions in new ventures they have attracted to the area, but only when there is a valid relationship between their own business and that of the new venture.

If the dismissal of protected employees becomes unavoidable, the employer should actively help them find suitable work elsewhere. The employer can provide financial bridging, pension portability, outplacement services, or retraining for those seeking new jobs; professional and financial assistance and subcontracts for those preferring self-employment. If the area suffers from a shortage of suitable jobs, the employer should do as much as possible to create or attract replacement jobs.

RECOMMENDATION 19

NOTES

1. Jerome M. Rosow and Robert Zager, *New Work Schedules for a Changing Society* (New York: Work in America Institute, 1981), pp. 98, 100.

2. Jerome M. Rosow and Robert Zager, *The Future of Older Workers in America* (New York: Work in America Institute, 1980), p. 73.

3. Bureau of Labor Statistics, U.S. Department of Labor, "Table 4—Civilian Labor Force Participation Rates by Race, Sex, and Age, 1974-79," in *Handbook of Labor Statistics*, Bulletin 2070 (Washington, D.C.: Bureau of Labor Statistics, Department of Labor, 1980).

4. Ronald Alsop, "As Early Retirement Grows in Popularity, Some Have Misgivings," *The Wall Street Journal*, April 24, 1984, p. 1+.

5. Ibid.

6. Charles Renfroe, "Job Sharing Is a Popular Option for Teachers, Others," *World of Work Report*, July 1982, p. 1.

7. Rosow and Zager, *New Work Schedules*, p. 99.

8. "Job Sharing, Swedish Style," *World of Work Report*, October 1980, p. 72.

9. Robert H. Guest, "Tarrytown: Quality of Work Life at a General Motors Plant," in *The Innovative Organization: Productivity Programs in Action*, edited by Robert Zager and Michael P. Rosow. Pergamon Press/Work in America Institute Series (New York: Pergamon Press, 1982), pp. 88-106.

10. Robert H. Guest, "The Sharonville Story: Worker Involvement at a Ford Motor Company Plant," in *The Innovative Organization: Productivity Programs in Action*, edited by Robert Zager and Michael P. Rosow. Pergamon Press/Work in America Institute Series (New York: Pergamon Press, 1982), pp. 44-62.

11. "Saving a Factory," *World of Work Report*, November 1983, p. 88.

12. a. "Pan Am Reaches Pacts on Wage Concessions with Three More Unions," *The Wall Street Journal*, December 23, 1982.

b. Agis Salpukas, "Cutting Airline Labor Costs: Job Shifts Aid Productivity," *The New York Times*, January 25, 1984.

c. Michael Brody, "Union Blues: More Managements Calling the Tune on Givebacks," *Barron's*, January 23, 1984.

13. Estimates by Dick Wright, director of Job Search Workshops, San Mateo, California, of JSW's achievements in self-directed job search.

14. William L. Batt, Jr., "Canada's Good Example with Displaced Workers," *Harvard Business Review* 61 (July-August 1983): 13-14.

15. a. "Blue-Collar Outplacement," *World of Work Report*, June 1980, p. 48.

b. "Helping Laid-Off Workers Find New Employment," *Chemical Engineering*, November 4, 1981, p. 55.

16. "New Growth Industry: Help for Fired Workers," *U.S. News and World Report*, August 1, 1983, p. 63.

17. Jill Casner-Lotto, "Retraining Displaced Workers Is Seen as Urgent Need," *World of Work Report*, January 1983, p. 6.

18. Jocelyn Gutchess, *Employment Security in Action: Strategies That Work*. Pergamon Press/Work in America Institute Series (New York: Pergamon Press, 1985).

19. Casner-Lotto, "Retraining Displaced Workers," p. 6.

20. Beverly Jacobson, *Young Programs for Older Workers*. Van Nostrand Reinhold/Work in America Institute Series (New York: Van Nostrand Reinhold, 1980), p. 17.

21. "Subcontracting: Be Your Own Boss," *The Economist*, June 4, 1983, p. 72.

22. Linda Wintner, *Employee Buyouts: An Alternative to Plant Closings* (New York: The Conference Board, 1983).

23. Joan Stableski, "Unions and Employee Ownership," *World of Work Report*, July 1983, p. 51.

24. Batt, "Canada's Good Example," pp. 20, 22.

25. Ibid., p. 22.

26. Ibid., p. 22.

27. Gutchess, *Employment Security in Action*.

28. William L. Batt, Jr., "British Steel et al.: In Plant Closings, Workers Are Important," *World of Work Report*, April 1981, pp. 28-29.

29. Gerard E. Watzke, "A European Alternative to Layoffs: Investment Incentives Offered by the Private Sector." Working Paper No. 143 (New Orleans: School of Business, Tulane University, 1982).

30. a. Ibid.

   b. Gutchess, *Employment Security in Action.*

7.
Alliances

Firms faced with imminent dismissals often cannot muster the energy, know-how, or resources to help their employees find new jobs. In recent years, a wide range of private and public institutions have emerged in the United States and Europe to fill that need. These organizations vary in composition, geographical scope, permanence, and functions. Some leading examples are the following:

☐ Trygghetsradet (Swedish Employment Security Council) is the most comprehensive. Formed in 1973 by the Employers' Federation (SAF) and the Federation of Salaried Employees in Industry and Services (PTK), the agency acts on behalf of thousands of employers and hundreds of thousands of employees. The council's original function was to ensure payment of severance pay to white-collar employees who were dismissed because of operational changes, with special assistance to older members of this group. Later, its activities expanded to include: helping dismissed employees search for a new job; "brokering" between companies that dismiss employees and those that need people; helping dismissed employees get training and education for new jobs; helping dismissed employees become self-employed; stimulating the establishment or expansion of small firms; and counseling member firms on how to reduce staff without dismissals.[1]

☐ Landskrona Finans Company (LAFI) is a Swedish public/ private agency owned by two towns, a state shipbuilding company, a regional investment firm, and 15 private industrial companies in the vicinity of the town of Landskrona. Although most of the capital is contributed by the state, the majority of votes are controlled by the private sector. The alliance was organized in 1981 to create replacements for the hundreds of jobs slated to be eliminated when the state shipyard closed in 1983.[2]

☐ Canada's Manpower Consultative Service (MCS) is a public agency, part of the federal government's Employment and Immigration unit. MCS intervenes when requested by firms and unions to help find jobs for employees about to be dismissed in a reduction in force (RIF) or closing. In 1980, 365 such interventions occurred, involving 200,000 workers; two-thirds of the participants obtained new jobs quickly.[3]

☐ The Plant Closure Response Unit was established in 1981, as part of the State of California's Employment Development Department. The unit is a task force comprised of representatives of business, labor, government, and education. Its function is to help out when plant shutdowns cause large-scale displacements. Given adequate lead time, it is able to respond quickly, coordinating the resources of employers, unions, economic development officials, job-service specialists, community colleges, and vocational education groups. As of January 1983, it had assisted in a dozen closings.[4]

☐ The California Employment Training Panel, created in 1983 by the governor and state legislature, retrains dismissed or about-to-be-dismissed employees. Headed by a joint labor-management board, it is financed by diverting $55 million a year that otherwise would have gone into the unemployment insurance system. The financing will continue for the four-year life of the program. As of mid-1984, $67.8 million had been committed, to train more than 20,000 people.[5]

☐ In Michigan, Rhode Island, and several other states, similar "economic adjustment teams" have rescued companies in trouble by restructuring businesses, finding new buyers, or arranging gradual relocation and retraining of displaced workers if a shutdown cannot be avoided.[6]

☐ Downriver Community Conference (DCC), created in the 1960s, is an alliance of 16 small communities in the heavily industrialized vicinity of Detroit, Michigan. Its original purpose was to resolve urban problems that the member communities could not manage alone. In 1979-80 it was confronted for the first time with several major plant closings that threw thousands of well-paid employees out of work. The organization responded with programs of social welfare, job-search assistance, retraining, and job creation.[7]

☐ In Munich, West Germany, an informal alliance of companies, unions, local governments, and the federal labor-market agency meets regularly five times a year to exchange information about employment-related problems in the area and to coordinate plans for dealing with them. Organized in 1982 to forestall a couple of major plant closings, the alliance has broadened its scope to include such matters as planning to provide training and apprenticeships for the annual influx of school leavers.[8]

☐ In Britain and Holland, a number of alliances have been formed by companies such as Pilkington Brothers, Philips, and Control Data to help create new jobs. These alliances may exist among private firms, between a firm and its local government, and between regional agencies and many firms.[9]

ALLIANCES IN ACTION

The principal activities in which alliances have engaged are outplacement, retraining, and job creation.

Outplacement

☐ Trygghetsradet maintains a personnel "clearing" function, analogous to check clearing among banks. When notified that employees are, or are about to become, redundant for operational reasons, the agency contacts its member companies to identify suitable vacancies for which the displaced employees might be eligible. If additional training is required, the council helps with financing. The displaced employee bears primary responsibility for conducting the job search, but the council's field workers supply guidance and moral support. (Although outsiders picture Sweden as a welfare state, the loss of a job is felt as keenly there as it is in the United States.)[10]

☐ Canada's Manpower Consultative Service (MCS) intervened in 1979, at the request of Disston Canada and the Steelworkers' local, when the firm's plant in Ontario announced that it would close in four months' time, displacing 110 hourly and 20 salaried employees. A joint manpower adjustment committee was set up, with an outside chairman. One hundred and one employees sought help, and within four months 90 had found suitable jobs. Committee expenses were shared by company, province, and federal government. The company, the union, and the committee chairman used their networks to uncover vacancies in the area. Employees were given time off for job interviews. Those who found jobs before the closing retained their entitlement to severance.

In 1980 MCS intervened in a 2,000-employee RIF at Ford Canada, in Oakville, Ontario. Separate committees were set up for hourly and salaried people, which met for eight months. Ninety-four percent of the participants found new jobs, despite the generally poor economic conditions, at a total cost of $60,000 (split among company, province, and federal government).[11]

Local committees set up by MCS can arrange counseling services, outplacement, training, and retraining; help with relocation; and investigate alternative assignments within the firm to prevent dismissals.[12]

☐ When Kaiser Steel announced plans to phase out its steelmaking facility over a one-year period, California's Plant Closure Response Unit helped the company and union officials to establish a reemployment center before massive layoffs occurred. Located on the company premises, the center provided job counseling, retraining, and placement assistance. Similarly, when General Electric announced the closing of its flatiron plant, vocational education classes were established for assembly-line workers before they were laid off. The classes were carefully structured to meet specific job openings in electronics and word processing.[13]

☐ Downriver Community Conference had to deal with 2,000 displaced employees from several large plant closings, some prior to shutdown, some after. All were offered help with immediate economic and social problems; then, after aptitude tests, they were enrolled in a four-day workshop in job-search skills (resumes, interviews, job applications, telephone techniques, and so on). People were then divided into three groups: those with a marketable skill went into job clubs; those without a marketable skill but high test scores were assigned to classroom technical training for high-level technical occupations; and the rest were designated for hands-on training, under contract, by small businesses. Considering the unusually high unemployment in the area, respectable placement rates were obtained.[14]

Retraining

☐ All training and education sponsored by Trygghetsradet is designed on an individual basis, with a specific job in view. A program may be as limited as the purchase of books or other literature, costing under $100, or as broad as a year of formal full-time education or training. The council sometimes pays travel expenses. If a dismissed employee has the training required for a particular occupation but is unfamiliar with its application to a firm which has an otherwise-suitable vacancy, the council may pay for the firm-specific training the individual receives after hiring. During training the employee receives state and council payments equivalent to about 70 percent of previous gross earnings. Some training is also provided to enable employees to fill future vacancies within the firm.[15]

☐ Downriver Community Conference contracted with community colleges for special condensed training programs; classes and lab periods were held at off-hours, five days a week, for nine months. Strongly motivated people with low test scores were given remedial reading and math and then allowed to take technical training. Subjects for courses were selected on the basis of DCC visits with local businesses, to find out what skills were needed. Then DCC negotiated with both businessmen and the community colleges to reach agreement on the detailed content of the courses. Among the courses provided were: numerically controlled machining, building-operations management, computer programming, industrial sales, word processing, and licensed practical nursing. Courses were conducted at three community colleges, one of which had four campuses. At the peak, 1,500 people were in classes.[16]

☐ All training under the aegis of the California Employment Training Panel is directed toward specific jobs: employers are committed to hire the trainees, and whoever does the training (whether an employer or an educational institution) is paid only if the trainees are actually hired and stay on the job at least 90 days. Employers and the panel share training costs. The panel works with business, labor, and training agencies to develop programs for high-demand, expanding fields. As of May 1984, 152 separate training contracts had been negotiated. Under one contract the California Manufacturers Association will retrain 1,000 ex-employees for jobs at member firms. Only good, steady jobs that pay above the minimum wage are considered. In some cases, trainees are employed from the start of training; more often, they remain on unemployment insurance until training is completed.[17]

Job Creation

□ Trygghetsradet offers 75 percent of severance pay, in cash, to dismissed employees who start a business of their own. About 10 percent of all dismissed employees become self-employed. A total of 2,000 companies have been launched, with 10,000 employees; sales amount to $500 million a year, with an average of $250,000. Forty percent are one-person firms; the others average eight persons per firm. Of those started in 1977, 70 percent still exist; of those started in 1980, 80 percent still exist.

The council awards scholarships to inventors to help them launch businesses. It has created an Inventors Academy, and it fosters university-industry relations. It also conducts regional seminars on new technology and venture capital.[18]

□ LAFI develops complete assistance "packages" to support new businesses getting started in the Landskrona area, but it supports only those that show promise of being successful and that are totally unrelated to shipbuilding. It provides financing, but only to supplement that obtained through normal channels. LAFI also takes some very conservative amounts of risk above those taken by the banks. Within two years, 63 companies and projects, providing 775 jobs in a wide range of manufacturing and commercial occupations, were operating under the LAFI umbrella.[19]

□ In response to the loss of 52 percent of primary jobs in its area, Downriver Community Conference inaugurated a federal procurement program to help small businesses obtain government contracts, mainly in defense. In 20 months of operation, it taught 700 Michigan firms how to bid. Eighty-one firms were successful, gaining 190 contracts worth a total of $41 million—90 percent with the Department of Defense.

DCC acts as broker, helping small firms get subcontracts from primary contractors. DCC's Small Business Development Center, which is sponsored by the U.S. Department of Commerce and the Small Business Administration, assists small firms in assembling information and paperwork, packaging loan applications to banks, and formulating marketing plans. In addition, DCC has set up "incubators" in an abandoned high school, where small businesses rent space for $3 to $4 a square foot, including central staff services for accounting, typing, phones, and the like.[20]

□ In the United Kingdom, Pilkington Brothers, a glass manufacturer, is allied with its local government, the St. Helen's District Council, to help in the formation of new enterprises and the expansion of local businesses. (Since 1979, over 100 new businesses have been formed, with about 2,000 jobs.[21]) The London Enterprise Agency, a group of 12 to 15 major firms, encourages private involvement in urban renewal. An even larger group, Business in the Community, has helped organize 150 agencies for the purpose of helping small businesses.[22]

One such agency, the New Work Trust, established a "workshop" in Bristol, where it has helped entrepreneurs launch 72 new businesses. The trust furnishes business services, training, marketing assistance, and help in introducing new technology. A second workshop is now being organized.[23]

□ In Holland, Philips Data Systems and The Hague formed a foundation to offer sites for new small businesses. The city provided the building; Philips provided funds for renovation. Together they engaged a United Kingdom consulting firm to contact and advise potential entrepreneurs; the consultant is paid according to the number of permanent jobs created. Control Data Corporation, Amro Bank, and several regional governments joined forces to encourage the development of new businesses in the city of Twente.[24]

Reducing Payroll without Dismissals

Upon invitation by a member company and union, Trygghetsradet serves as consultant and funding agent to help avoid dismissals when a RIF becomes necessary. The council organizes a high-level union-management project committee, assists the committee in reaching agreement on the required reduction, and then helps it devise a program to achieve the reduction with the smallest number of dismissals. Whenever possible, employees who leave by attrition are not replaced, and the only people hired are those with essential new skills. The project committee determines where future vacancies will occur in the firm and invites redundant employees to apply for and/or train for them. Redundant employees leave their current jobs at once, so that the company can quickly assume its streamlined configuration. Actions are tailored to the needs of each dismissed employee. A few may retire early; some become self-employed, with training and assistance from the council; others are trained and helped to get outside jobs. Several employees may resign voluntarily. The firm's cost in a dismissal-prevention project is roughly equal to the cost it would incur if the RIF were accomplished by dismissals.[25]

Other Possible Uses for Alliances

Regional Job Banks. The process of helping displaced employees find new jobs is hindered by the absence of a federal-state employment service system that enjoys the confidence of employers. Employers refuse to list with the employment service any but their most pedestrian vacancies. When a RIF threatens, a company seeking to help its employees must start from square one. Unfortunately, there is no hope that the lack of confidence will be repaired any time in the foreseeable future.

The experience of Trygghetsradet and the Munich alliance shows the advantages of privately controlled job clearinghouses, even in countries where employers are required to register vacancies with the state employment service. The experience of many U.S. companies that have conducted outplacement programs—some in alliance with state plant-closure task forces—shows that employers will cooperate in ad hoc job clearinghouses, provided there is no governmental coercion.

Voluntary job clearinghouses could be established on a permanent basis at no great cost. They would speed the rehiring of displaced employees both in large-scale RIFs and in the many small day-to-day dismissals that are bound to occur in a dynamic economy. Employers would benefit in two ways: (1) their unemployment insurance taxes would be lower because of the reduction of "frictional" unemployment; and (2) they would gain access to a supply of proven employees to fill their vacancies.

Once in full operation, a clearinghouse might expand into related brokerage functions. For example, it might help in transferring a dismissed employee's pension rights to the new employer's plan. Or, if an employee is prepared to take a pay cut in order to land a new job, it might arrange for the former employer to make up at least part of the shortfall. Or it might negotiate with the former employer to pay the new employer to retrain a dismissed employee.

Employers and local and international unions in a metropolitan area or a major industrial region should band together to organize a computer-based job clearinghouse and keep it up to date. Where an area labor-management committee already exists, it should take an active part in this effort.

Retraining. To develop a training program for one person costs the same as for 100. To administer a training program for one person costs roughly the same as for a full-sized class of 15, 20, or 30. Thus, for practical purposes, the larger the number of people to be retrained in a given subject, the lower the cost per trainee.

While a very large RIF may displace enough employees to allow economies of scale in retraining, most dismissals are not of such magnitude. To deal with normal situations, firms in the same industrial region can pool their resources to reduce the costs and broaden the diversity of available retraining programs. (A group of firms in the Jamestown [N.Y.] Area Labor-Management Committee reportedly had such an arrangement.) Downriver Community Conference has demonstrated that pooling helps even when fairly large RIFs take place in several firms at the same time.

The pooling firms need not set up their own retraining programs. Increasingly, giant enterprises as well as smaller ones are contracting for the flexible facilities of community colleges and other postsecondary schools. The institutions courted this market originally to compensate for the clientele lost at the end of the baby boom, but they now see it as a permanent source of demand.

Regional groups of employers and unions, both local and international, should form alliances to provide retraining and education for employees who have lost jobs through no fault of their own. To gain flexibility and economy, the allies should avail themselves of the services of postsecondary schools.

Long-term alliances between businesses and postsecondary schools have also proved useful. The productivity improvement collaboration between a supplier of carburetors to General Motors, located in Tuscaloosa, Alabama, and the University of Alabama was mentioned in chapter 6. And in the field of training (as distinguished from retraining), industry and education have begun to "contract out" with each other. For example, in Michigan, local industry sends employees to Bay de Noc Community College for occupational training. In Wisconsin, the Milwaukee Technical School sends instructors into the factory to upgrade the skills of workers. The potential for such integration has barely been tapped so far.[26]

Job Creation. Many locales in the United States are heavily dependent on a single industry, or on one or a few large employers, as the source of jobs. In such areas one industry's temporary or permanent decline of demand can cause havoc, compelling individuals and businesses to seek more government intervention than they would otherwise consider desirable. Yet, when times are good and jobs appear secure, no one wants to bother with correcting the imbalance. Only after hardship strikes are job-creating programs organized. And since jobs cannot be created overnight, suffering is often long and intense.

It is now an accepted fact that most new jobs are created by small, rather than large, businesses. Four qualifying facts need to be borne in mind: (1) small firms have a brief half-life—on average, jobs in small firms go out of existence almost, but not quite, as fast as they are born, (2) many small firms are units of large ones, owned and controlled elsewhere, (3) small firms, in general, offer less attractive pay, benefits, and security than large firms, in general, and (4) if a small firm serves only a local market, its ups and downs of employment merely amplify those that already dominate the area.

Employers, local and international unions, and local and state governments should form alliances to diversify the job base in areas where employment depends heavily on the fortunes of a single industry or a few firms. They should try to  **RECOMMENDATION 22**

attract small firms that (1) demonstrate potential for growth, (2) are industrially diverse and have economic cycles that differ from those that prevail in the area, and (3) find a large part of their market at a safe distance from the work site. Alliances should also include those union-management pension funds over whose investment policies the unions exercise some control. Such funds have billions of dollars in assets and would like to invest a portion in ventures to create jobs for union members. Governments should assist by enabling the pension funds to make such investments, subject to limited gains and limited risks.

NOTES

1. Remarks by Hans Ursing at a meeting of the National Advisory Committee for "Employment Security in a Free Economy," a Work in America Institute policy study, in Dearborn, Michigan, November 10, 1984. Also, Eric Peterson and Ulf Eriksson, "Assessment of the Swedish Employment Security Council's Dismissal Prevention Activities," an unpublished progress report prepared for Trygghetsradet, Stockholm, Sweden, September 14, 1983, and *The SAF-PTK Employment Security Council* (Stockholm, Sweden: Trygghetsradet SAF-PTK, 1980).

2. Jocelyn F. Gutchess, *Employment Security in Action: Strategies That Work.* Pergamon Press/Work in America Institute Series (New York: Pergamon Press, 1985).

3. William L. Batt, Jr., "Canada's Good Example with Displaced Workers," *Harvard Business Review* 61 (July-August 1983): 8.

4. Jill Casner-Lotto, "Retraining Displaced Workers Is Seen as Urgent Need," *World of Work Report*, January 1983, p. 7.

5. Gutchess, *Employment Security in Action.*

6. "Saving Plants and Jobs," *World of Work Report*, June 1984, p. 3.

7. Remarks by Freda Rutherford at a meeting of the National Advisory Committee for "Employment Security in a Free Economy," a Work in America Institute policy study, in Dearborn, Michigan, November 10, 1984. Also "The Programs of the Downriver Community Conference," an unpublished paper commissioned by Work in America Institute, October 1983.

8. Gutchess, *Employment Security in Action.*

9. Gerard E. Watzke, "A European Alternative to Layoffs:

Incentives Offered by the Private Sector." Working Paper No. 143 (New Orleans: School of Business, Tulane University, 1982).

10. Remarks by Hans Ursing at a meeting of the National Advisory Committee for "Employment Security in a Free Economy," November 10, 1983, and papers noted above.

11. Batt, "Canada's Good Example," p. 8.

12. Gutchess, *Employment Security in Action.*

13. Casner-Lotto, "Retraining Displaced Workers, p. 7.

14. Remarks by Freda Rutherford at a meeting of the National Advisory Committee for "Employment Security in a Free Economy," November 10, 1983, and the paper noted above.

15. Remarks by Hans Ursing at a meeting of the National Advisory Committee for "Employment Security in a Free Economy," November 10, 1983, and papers noted above.

16. Remarks by Freda Rutherford at a meeting of the National Advisory Committee for "Employment Security in a Free Economy," November 10, 1983, and the paper noted above.

17. Gutchess, *Employment Security in Action.*

18. Remarks by Hans Ursing at a meeting of the National Advisory Committee for "Employment Security in a Free Economy," and papers noted above.

19. Gutchess, *Employment Security in Action.*

20. Remarks by Freda Rutherford at a meeting of the National Advisory Committee for "Employment Security in a Free Economy," and the paper noted above.

21. Gutchess, *Employment Security in Action.*

22. Gerard E. Watzke, "A European Alternative to Layoffs."

23. Gutchess, *Employment Security in Action.*

24. Watzke, "A European Alternative to Layoffs."

25. Eric Petersson and Ulf Eriksson, "Assessment of the Swedish Employment Security Council's Dismissal Prevention Activities," an unpublished progress report prepared for Trygghetsradet, Stockholm, Sweden, September 14, 1983.

26. Remarks by Paul Barton, quoted in Casner-Lotto, "Retraining Displaced Workers," p. 7.

8.
A Supportive Role for Government

In view of the potential advantages of employment security for the national economy, and in view of the social costs of unemployment, one might expect the federal government to lend its support. Instead, federal policies work strongly and consistently against employment security, reinforcing what has been aptly called a "neutron bomb" mindset among employers; that is, preserve physical assets, but zap the people who operate them.

The government can begin to reverse these disincentives by treating physical and human assets equally. And since economic recessions are the greatest single threat to employment security, government policy needs to find ways of assisting employers who try to make good on their commitments. (Federal policies for full employment, however, are not within the scope of this report, as noted on pp. 22-23.)

As against the federal government's disheartening behavior, several states have enacted short-time compensation (STC) laws that make work sharing more attractive as an alternative to layoff. In 1982, Congress, to its credit, provided some low-cost support to this progress by directing the secretary of labor to provide model legislation and technical aid to states interested in adopting STC.

NEUTRALIZING "NEUTRON BOMB" POLICIES

Federal policies consistently reward employers for investing in physical assets but discourage them from investing in people. Human assets consist of skill, experience, problem-solving ability, and loyalty. Much of any employee's "capital" is specific to the employer and not readily transferable. Increasingly, skills come through specialized training, especially in connection with new technology. Although people are the only asset that *grows* in value, the system of unemployment insurance undercuts these assets by favoring layoffs and dismissals as against efforts to keep surplus employees on the payroll.

How the "Bomb" Works

These are some of the ways in which the federal government discourages employment security.

Discriminatory Tax Treatment. Through favorable tax treatment, the federal government encourages hostile mergers, acquisitions, and leveraged buyouts, all of which are notoriously harmful to employment security. Such changes of ownership and control create no new physical assets. When, as often happens, the purpose is to sell off the less-profitable parts of the acquired business or reduce staffing at all levels, the new owners show less compunction than the old ones about the fate of the displaced employees. In fact, the new owners are making a capital acquisition and not an acquisition of human talent. As far as the federal government is concerned, the new owners have carte blanche. Nothing matters but "mobility of capital."

Writeoffs. When an employer liquidates physical assets, as in the closure of an obsolete plant, the tax laws allow it to offset against current profits any capital loss thus incurred, or to carry the loss forward to offset future profits. If a corporation with such a loss is sold to a profitable company, the purchaser acquires the right to offset that loss against its own future profits. The loss is transformed into an asset. The write-offs represent (1) the residual value of the assets, and (2) the costs of guarding and maintaining the assets during the period of disposition. Physical assets are an investment in the expectation of future earnings.

An individual's continued service with an employer similarly represents an investment in the expectation of future earnings. When an employee is dismissed without fault, this expectation is not met and the employee may sustain severe losses. Typical losses suffered by employees include wages and benefits that would have been earned if the job had continued minus wages and benefits received on a replacement job minus any unemployment insurance benefits actually received; the costs of retraining for a new job; and so on. Unlike an employer, a dismissed employee cannot offset the losses against future earnings; they must be borne when they are hardest to bear.

Import Protection. When the government grants import protection to an industry, one ostensible reason is to protect American jobs by giving the industry breathing space to become more competitive. Part of becoming more competitive is to make better use of human assets, and this implies a reasonable degree of employment security. Although every firm in the designated industry enjoys protection, none is required to do anything about becoming more competitive. When the period ends, many employees find themselves no better off than before, and many are jobless.

Trade Adjustment Assistance Benefits. Out of general revenues, the government pays Trade Adjustment Assistance (TAA) benefits to workers displaced by imports, without regard to whether they are preparing themselves for jobs in other industries, and without trying to counsel them about the need for, or the methods of, preparing themselves. Counseling is essential because many displaced workers become emotionally distressed and refuse (sometimes with good reason) to believe that their jobs are actually going out of existence. Payments to workers are sup-

Table 1
Trade Adjustment Assistance Benefits, 1975-1981

	Workers Applying for Certification (one thousand)	Workers Certified (one thousand)	Total Benefits Paid ($1 million)
1975	122	46.9	13.5
1976	430	62.3	70.4
1977	411	110.7	151.9
1978	853	155.7	263.1
1979	844	132.2	265.9
1980	935	531.7	1,652.0
1981	333	27.8	1,441.1

Source: Office of Trade Adjustment Assistance, U.S. Department of Labor, Washington, D.C.

posed to help them retrain for, obtain, and relocate to new jobs. But, as tables 1 and 2 show, not even one-half of one percent of the benefits have been applied to those activities. The payments have merely supplemented unemployment insurance benefits; they have delayed, rather than encouraged, efforts to find new jobs. Some recipients have even held out long enough to be recalled by their old employers, exactly the opposite of what was intended. Others have been discouraged from taking jobs when the after-tax earnings were near the level of benefits for not working.

In Japan, by contrast, when an industry loses international competitiveness and large-scale dismissals become necessary, the firms and their unions assume primary responsibility for retraining and outplacing the displaced workers to new and growing sectors of the economy.

Export Subsidies. In the name of increasing domestic employment, the government grants export subsidies out of general revenues. The grants are given without regard to whether the subsidized employers make any effort to become more competitive or to provide employment security.

Government Contracts. The government issues large contracts to thousands of employers who have to meet stiff conditions regarding equal employment opportunity and other government programs. Typically, however, people hired to carry out a government contract are dismissed as soon as the contract is completed,

Table 2
Breakdowns of U.S. Trade Adjustment Assistance
Benefits, 1976-1980
(in $1 million)

	Weekly Benefits	Relocation	Job Search	Job Training
1976	69.9	.05	.01	.47
1977	150.8	.25	.03	.84
1978	258.3	.60	.16	4.04
1979	258.1	1.17	.31	6.36
1980	1,644.9	.61	.11	6.41

Source: Same as Table 1

often with little or no advance notice, and almost always without help in finding a new job.

Rapid Depreciation of Capital Investments. In order to spur investment and help employers become more competitive, the government allows rapid depreciation of capital investments at the expense of the general taxpayer. If a new investment causes displacement of employees, as often happens, the company may dispose of the employees as it sees fit.

Pension Policies. The government makes it profitable for employers to dismiss employees whose pensions have not yet been vested. When an employee leaves the firm prior to vesting, even if without fault, the money paid into the pension fund on behalf of that employee remains behind, in the fund, even though pension contributions are deferred compensation. When there is a reduction in force, the company may enjoy a bonanza, since it is able, through changing actuarial assumptions, to appropriate the plan's excess funds for general corporate use. This practice is contrary to the national interest since the government finances about half of pension costs through tax policy. Now many companies have begun to "cash out" their defined benefit plans by shifting to profit sharing or defined contributions—thereby transferring large sums to corporate assets.

In July 1984, a bill was introduced in the Senate, which would require that employees be able to take their pensions with them when they change jobs, either by transferring benefits to the new employer or by rolling them over into an IRA.

Lack of Severance Requirements. The government does not require employers to pay severance to employees dismissed without fault. Even when an employer agrees to pay severance, it can get off the hook by keeping employees on indefinite layoff until they give up and take other jobs. Only collective agreements protect severance payments as a right. Therefore, for many employees, years of dedicated company service have no economic value at time of dismissal—the very time when the need is most intense.

We recommend that Congress establish a more rational balance between capital mobility and employment security, through the following actions:

1. Federal tax policy should be redefined to recognize the funda-

mental rights of every citizen to tax protection against economic hardship, such as unemployment. Further, tax policy should treat individuals and families with a more reasonable degree of equity as compared to corporations.

2. When employers seek favorable tax treatment in a merger, acquisition, or leveraged buyout, they should be required to show that they have provided appropriately for the security of regular employees who, through no fault of their own, have been downgraded or made surplus as a result of the transaction.

3. Employers should be allowed to take tax write-offs and credits against future income (a) for expenses incurred in keeping surplus employees on the payroll during a temporary business decline, and (b) for expenses incurred in helping dismissed employees retrain for, obtain, and relocate to new jobs. Employees dismissed without fault should be allowed tax credits against future income for (a) earnings and benefits lost between dismissal and reemployment, (b) any decrease of earnings and benefits between old and new jobs, and (c) costs incurred in retraining for, obtaining, and relocating to a new job.

4. When employers seek import protection or export subsidies, they should be required to show that they have provided appropriately for the security of regular employees who, through no fault of their own, may be downgraded or made surplus while the employers are enjoying such federal assistance.

5. Trade Adjustment Assistance (TAA) should be paid only to employees who are taking positive steps to obtain jobs in other industries (training, education, or relocation). However, the federal and state governments should counsel TAA-eligibles with regard to (a) the likelihood of exhausting benefits before being rehired, (b) the kinds of preparation needed in order to enter an occupation that is likely to remain in demand, and (c) local sources of education and training.

6. When employers submit a proposal for a major government contract, they should be required to make appropriate provision for the security of employees (other than those hired as temporaries) who are hired to perform the contract and who, at the expiration of the contract, are downgraded or made surplus through no fault of their own.

7. When employers claim accelerated depreciation of physical assets, they should be required to show that they have provided appropriately for the security of regular employees who, through no fault of their own, were downgraded or made surplus as a result of the introduction of those assets.

8. *The rules of ERISA should be amended to provide that when employees are dismissed through no fault of their own, they do not lose their unvested pension rights. If an employer's pension plan does not already make such provisions, employer and employee should be required to work out a mutually agreeable arrangement for the employee to retain such rights in the plan until retirement, or to transfer them into the next employer's pension plan, an IRA, or a similar deferred-compensation account.*

9. *All employers should be required to pay a reasonable amount of severance to employees who, without fault, either are dismissed or laid off for 12 months or more. Preferably, severance pay should be service-based at the minimum level of one week for every year of service.*

BROADENING THE CONCEPT OF UNEMPLOYMENT INSURANCE

The federal/state system of unemployment insurance was designed to provide income security, not employment security. Its application has, in fact, operated *against* employment security, by encouraging overreliance on layoffs and dismissals as the prime means of reducing payroll costs. A countermovement, in the form of state legislation to permit short-time compensation (STC), was initiated by California in 1978 and has spread to Oregon, Arizona, Florida, Illinois, Washington, and Maryland. Although still a device for income security, STC promotes employment security by spreading the available work over the greatest number of employees and avoiding layoffs.[1]

California modeled its statute on West Germany's, although many other countries—Belgium, France, Italy, Great Britain, Luxembourg, Denmark, the Netherlands, Norway, Australia, and Canada—also have STC laws. The West German plan has been in operation almost 60 years and is considered the most successful of all. During the 1974-75 recession, 77,000 German workers were on STC, reducing the overall unemployment rate by approximately one percentage point. During the 1980-82 recession, over half a million employees were drawing STC benefits.

A West German firm becomes eligible for STC by demonstrating that a reduction in hours of labor is unavoidable and that work-time reductions with STC will prevent dismissals. Employers must also document that work-time reductions of at least 10 percent have already been made for at least one-third of their employees for a period of four continuous weeks. Firms and industries judged to be in permanent decline rather than in temporary recession are usually denied eligibility.

Decisions to reduce work time (or lay workers off) must be reached by agreement between the employer and the works council (which represents all strata of employees, union and non-union). If the works council consents, the program becomes binding upon all affected workers. Dissenting workers can avoid the shorter workweek only by resigning.

Benefits are paid directly by the firm to its employees, and the government reimburses the firm. The benefits have a ceiling but are free of tax, so that take-home earnings are maintained at 80 percent to 90 percent of regular earnings. The firm must provide fringe benefits throughout. Normally, STC can be drawn for up to six months, but the period can be extended for as much as two years. The typical STC recipient undergoes a work-time reduction of about 40 percent (two days a week) and draws benefits less than three months.

The West German program must be viewed in perspective. European restraints on layoff are much tougher than in the United States. Large parts of European fringe-benefit programs are administered by the government, which reduces the fixed costs of labor. Finally, unemployment benefit ceilings are considerably higher than those of most American states.

The California Law

The first state program for STC in the United States was adopted by California in 1978, a month before the passage of Proposition 13. The program was given a one-year trial and then extended in 1979 for a second year.

California's program offers partial benefits for up to 20 weeks a year to workers whose companies put them on short time in order to avoid a layoff. Benefits are proportional to regular unemployment insurance benefits. For example, a worker who would be entitled to $100 for a full week of unemployment would receive $20 for being unemployed one day a week. Since unemployment insurance benefits are tax free and the worker is freed of job-related costs, such as transportation and lunch, most work sharers in California end up with about 90 percent of take-home pay.

Both the firm and its workers have to meet regular California unemployment insurance eligibility requirements. The employer must state in writing that the firm wishes to participate, declaring that a reduction of work hours in all or part of the establishment is necessary to avoid layoff. Normal work hours must be reduced at least 10 percent a week for at least 10 percent of the regular permanent work force in the affected unit or units. If employees are represented by a union, the union must consent to the plan. The employer may or may not continue fringe benefits. If participating workers moonlight or work in excess of the planned work time, the extra earnings are deducted from their short-time compensation benefits.

Workers on STC remain eligible for regular unemployment insurance benefits if they are subsequently laid off. However, the total of short-time compensation and regular benefits per year cannot exceed the amount they would have been entitled to under regular unemployment insurance.

Employers with a history of heavy use of layoffs, who are already paying maximum tax under the regular unemployment insurance program, must pay a penalty tax in order to participate in STC. A number of firms have made use of STC despite this extra cost.

Between July 1978 and September 1980, over 1,290 employer plans, covering 35,300 employees, were approved. Some 16,280 claims were paid, and claimants received payment, on average, for one day's employment per week, for a period of five weeks.

Twelve percent of the plans included employees covered by a collective bargaining agreement, and 22 percent of all employees approved for participation in the program worked for unionized employers.

A limited telephone survey in December 1979 found generally favorable reactions. Of 30 employers who had used the program, 25 favored it strongly; 5 were neutral. Those favoring the program asserted that it helped them retain valued employees, was generally appreciated by employees, and was easy and flexible to administer. Twenty representatives of participating local unions also responded; of these, 14 favored the program, 3 were neutral or unaware of the program, and 3 had not actually been involved. Advantages cited for the program were that work sharing is more equitable than layoffs, that workers are better off financially, and that fringe benefits are maintained (although the employer is not required to do so by law). Four unions had encountered resistance from members at first, which gradually diminished.[2]

Since this information was published in 1981, additional information about STC in West Germany, California, and Canada has been gathered. (The Canadian statute went into effect in 1978). For a comparison of the three programs see table 2 in the appendix.

West Germany. Unemployment insurance is funded by equal contributions of employer and employees, totaling 4.6 percent of wages. STC replaces two-thirds of the net income lost by the worker; but payments are reduced by 50 percent of any net outside income. At the end of 1982, legislation extended STC payments for the steel industry to 36 months, for the years 1983-84. In January 1983, 1,190,397 employees were on short-time compensation, thus reducing the country's serious unemployment problem.[3]

California. An evaluation commissioned by the state, covering the period from 1978 through December 1982, reported that:

☐ A total of 4,300 firms and 174,000 employees had been approved for participation. In 1982 alone, 1,970 firms and 82,000 workers were approved. Even so, STC accounted for only 0.5 percent of all 1982 unemployment insurance claims in the state, reducing unemployment by 20,000. The figure would have been higher, but many employers bypassed STC because they believed the recession would last well beyond the 20-week limit of STC and they would eventually have to dismiss people anyway. (In 1983, when the law was renewed to run through 1986, the limit was raised to 26 consecutive weeks.)

☐ Over 50 percent of the firms whose employees received short-time compensation were in manufacturing, as compared to 11 percent of the firms whose employees claimed regular unemployment insurance. The proportion of unionized firms and workers using STC was about the same as for regular unemployment compensation.

☐ Eighty-nine percent of participating employers chose STC because they "desired to retain valued employees." Full-time labor costs were reduced more by STC than they would have been by a comparable number of layoffs. Other advantages noted were: higher morale and motivation; better union-management relations; and more efficient use of equipment and resources. Ninety-three percent of participating employers said they would use it again, if the need arose.

☐ What the participating workers valued most were: employment security; more equitable distribution of hardship; more free time. Ninety percent of them said they would chose it again, if necessary.

☐ The direct cost of STC to the state was probably a little higher than that of unemployment insurance.[4]

Canada. Canada's STC law differs in important particulars from California's. First, unemployment insurance benefits are much higher in Canada, so senior workers are less opposed to STC. Second, duration is 52 weeks. Third, the system does not use experience rating; the firm pays two-thirds, the government pays one-third.

☐ The Canadian program began slowly, but between December 1981 and February 1983, over 11,000 firms and almost 233,000 employees were approved to participate, with the result that 98,500 full-time layoffs were avoided. Yet the number of STC claimants in 1982 was less than 1.5 percent of those claiming regular unemployment insurance.

☐ Seventy-one percent of Canadian firms using STC were in manufacturing and 39 percent of firms were unionized, as compared with 50 percent and 14 percent in California. However, reactions of Canadian employers and employees to the pros and cons of STC were virtually identical to those in California.[5]

RECOMMENDATION 24 ► *We recommend that employers and local and international unions jointly lobby for STC laws in those states that have not yet adopted them.*

New Applications for STC

As STC spreads, innovative applications will suggest themselves. For example, suppose that employees on STC volunteer to participate in their employer's training programs during STC hours. As long as an employer is willing to pay the costs of training, and the employees on STC are willing to invest their free time, would it not be preferable to use that time to the advantage of the economy, the employer, and the employees instead of paying people to do nothing? The impact on the unemployment insurance fund would be no greater than that of STC alone.

One objection to combining STC with training in the past has been that it was forbidden by law. However, a mandatory federal standard enacted in 1970 declares that no state may deny unemployment insurance benefits to a claimant who has enrolled in an approved training program, even if this renders the claimant "unavailable for work." Although the states have conformed on paper, most have merely granted a right of *appeal*. The procedure is of minimal value, however, because very few unemployed workers have ever heard about the training option. A few states have taken positive steps:

☐ Delaware has launched a pilot program of educational vouchers that entitle unemployed workers to obtain (1) job counseling, and (2) retraining at vocational schools and community colleges. By selecting claimants who are unlikely to find a job before their benefits run out, the state hopes to cut unemployment insurance costs. The state's employment service staff has been trained to counsel claimants, tell them whether they have any hope of being reemployed in their current occupation, and advise them about the availability of educational services.[6]

☐ Arizona has paid up to six months of schooling to retrain unemployed copper workers.[7]

☐ California has established an Employment Training Fund to train unemployed people for new occupations. The fund consists of $55 million a year that otherwise would have gone into the unemployment insurance system and offers a wide variety of effective programs.[8]

Since unemployment insurance can legally be applied to on-the-job training, so can STC. Canada has shown the way:

> Workers can now use their work-sharing days for on-the-job training, and the federal government will pay the employer for a major portion of the training and administrative costs. The employer provides the worker with training at the work site, in a classroom, or in a special training area. Employees who take advantage of this training opportunity will obviously improve their chances of retaining their present jobs or of finding new ones. There is a benefit to the employer,

too. While on work sharing, employers have embarked on new marketing or sales initiatives to help them out of their difficulties. Some have also taken the opportunity to improve or upgrade their production equipment and/or processes. If these improvements necessitate skills upgrading by some or all employees in the work unit, the reduction in the work week provides an ideal opportunity for this to occur. . . . A management/labor committee is formed to plan training assistance for the affected workers.[9]

On-the-job training for employees on STC is a valid social policy, as Employment and Immigration Canada asserts, because it makes people more valuable to their current and future employers, and thereby less likely to become future charges on provincial or federal taxpayers. The same case can be made for literacy training, remedial education, and acquisition of the general equivalency diploma (GED). As technology advances, fewer and fewer desirable jobs are open to individuals who lack basic intellectual skills. Even low-tech jobs now require them. Yet tens of millions of youths and adults in the United States are functionally illiterate, and millions of others lack either a high school or a general equivalency diploma. These disadvantaged people are among the most susceptible to layoff and the least adaptable to technological change. A combination of STC and basic education would be a sound investment for all concerned.

Conversely, employees on STC might also be permitted to enroll in approved courses of skill development or continuing education at vocational schools, technical schools, community colleges, adult education programs, or four-year institutions. Many employers already offer to pay tuition for employees who pursue education and training on their own time, provided that the courses are relevant to the employee's regular job, but surprisingly few employees accept. Perhaps utilization would increase if employers liberalized the benefits and the criteria of relevance for those on STC.

The concept of STC for on-the-job training suggests a still more fruitful application. When an employer lays people off, or enters into an STC program with them, this action does not indicate that the employees in question have no current value to the employer. It indicates only that the value they can generate at the current rate of production is less than the cost of keeping them on the payroll. Frequently the employer has other useful work that needs to be done, which those employees could do, and for which the employer could afford to pay 40, 50, or 60 percent of the regular wage. For example, these tasks might include deferred mechanical or building maintenance, or reconstruction of customers' used machines (such as IBM's typewriters or Lincoln Electric's welding machines). If the surplus employees are willing to do the offered work, and if STC could be paid in such a case, everybody—including the state and federal governments—would benefit. The mechanics of this application may present difficulties but, if they can be worked out, the potential is very great. The employer's work force would be held together, with less strain between senior and junior employees during temporary declines; the employer would get useful work done without losing money on it; the gross national product would be increased; and the cost to unemployment insurance funds would be no more than for STC.

STC might be useful also to maintain work-force cohesiveness and morale during the traumatic period when employees are receiving outplacement assistance. (Such an extension of STC has, in fact, been introduced in Canada.) In principle, STC should be given only when a workplace suffers a temporary loss of demand and employees are expected to return to full schedules within a reasonable time. Otherwise, STC would merely delay the inevitable adjustments, and the state would have to support employer and employees indefinitely. However, if an outplacement program is under way, this objection does not arise: STC, by relieving employees' anxieties and allowing them to concentrate on the task at hand, might accelerate rather than retard the adjustment.

We recommend that employers and local and international unions jointly lobby Congress and the legislatures of STC states to make STC payable for a limited period to otherwise-eligible employees during unpaid hours (1) for voluntary on-*the-job training, (2) for remedial education, (3) for skill development or continuing education, (4) for supplementing the partial wages of employees who perform work which is substantially less valuable than their normal work, and (5) when they are receiving outplacement assistance.*

RECOMMENDATION
25

EMPLOYMENT SECURITY AND GENERAL RECESSION

Employers that commit themselves to employment security against business declines face one almost incalculable risk: general recession. Whatever the precipitating cause, a recession cannot occur except as a result of the monetary and fiscal policies approved by the President, Congress, and the Federal Reserve Board. How long and deep the decline will be is determined by the combined economic effects of these policies, which often exceed the intentions of the policy makers. There is nothing an employer can do to prevent the adverse effects of a national recession. Therefore, even the strongest company may be forced to renege on or modify its commitment to employment security.

Although it is *de rigueur* for policy reports to urge the federal government to end stop-and-go economic management and strive for full employment, the record contains no evidence that the recommendation has ever been heeded. We take a realistic course and urge the government at least to repair some of the havoc recessions cause—especially the economic hardships imposed upon individuals and the loss of human capital to the economy.

The federal government should assist employers who have given an explicit commitment of employment security against business declines. The assistance should consist of reimbursement for the net additional costs they incur as a result of retaining employees instead of laying them off or dismissing them during a recession. This federal subsidy of employment security will require time and financial limits. However, the gross costs will be offset by savings in income-transfer and retraining programs, and by the continuation of tax revenues from employed workers.

NOTES

1. Ramelle MaCoy and Martin J. Morand, eds., *Short-Time Compensation: A Formula for Work Sharing.* Pergamon Press/ Work in America Institute Series (New York: Pergamon Press, 1984).

2. Jerome M. Rosow and Robert Zager, *New Work Schedules for a Changing Society* (New York: Work in America Institute, 1981), pp. 93-96.

3. "International Short-Time and Layoffs," *European Industrial Relations Review*, April 1983, pp. 15-19.

4. Fred Best, "Short-Time Compensation in North America: Trends and Prospects," an unpublished paper commissioned by Work in America Institute, March 15, 1983.

5. Ibid.

6. Paul E. Barton, "Skill Development: Alternatives to Layoffs and Income Maintenance," an unpublished paper commissioned by Work in America Institute, March 1983.

7. a. Ibid.

   b. Judith Cummings, "Novel Ways Being Used to Save Jobs," *The New York Times*, January 28, 1983.

8. a. Jill Casner-Lotto, "Retraining: California's Novel Approach," *World of Work Report*, July 1984, pp. 1-2.

   b. Jocelyn Gutchess, *Employment Security in Action: Strategies That Work*. Pergamon Press/Work in America Institute Series (New York: Pergamon Press, 1985).

9. Employment and Immigration Canada, *Work Sharing: An Alternative to Temporary Layoffs* (Ottawa, Ontario: Employment and Immigration Canada, 1983).

Appendix

Table 1

Types of Employer-Provided Employment Stabilization Programs

	Nature of Employer Obligation or Guarantee	Coverage and Eligibility Conditions	Conditions to Void or Modify the Guarantee	Corollary Employers' Policies/Programs/Buffers	Corollary Legal and Cultural Factors	Selected Experience
1. *"Lifetime" employment in socialist countries—various*	Legal obligations to provide employment indefinitely, except for those who work under stated contract terms.	All workers, following a probationary period.	Individual dismissals and layoffs possible in several circumstances: e.g., enterprise is being closed; operations to be curtailed; individual employee is incompetent, absent, commits crime, or neglects duties.	Severance pay required in cases of reductions in force.	Centralized national planning and control of economy. Labor market compulsion.	Some overstaffing and some excessive turnover. Low productivity (e.g., U.S.S.R.)
2. *"Lifetime" employment—Japan*	Moral obligations reinforced by cultural norms.	Regular, male employees of large organizations. Estimates of coverage range from 10% to 35% of the total work force.	Termination after probationary period only for major criminal offenses.	Once-per-year hiring of school graduates (high school and university). Early retirement at 55, currently rising to 60 in many countries. Long orientation period, followed by broad-based training.	Legislation passed in 1977 provides some financial assistance to employees to help maintain lifetime employment. Extreme use of subcontracting firms.	As society grows older, there is some concern that the policy will have to be modified. Enterprise unions.

Wide use of temporary employees and women, who do not have lifetime employment rights.

Large share of compensation paid in the form of bonuses. When firm is not too successful, bonuses are low.

Promotions both by seniority and by merit. Salary increases mainly by seniority.

Tendency toward paternalism.

Premise is that employees are more important than earning money.

Severance payments required. (In Mexico, e.g., 3 months' wages and 12 days' pay year of service).

Dismissals and layoffs possible: for cause (dishonesty, malfeasance, misfeasance) and for retrenchment pur-

Employer must demonstrate to a government board that the layoff is planned for appropriate, legally approved reasons.

Tendency to use temporaries who do not attain the legal rights available to "permanent" employees.

All noncontract employees.

Legal obligation to encourage permanent employment.

3. *Employment guaranteed by law (e.g., Mexico)*

Table 1 (continued)

	Nature of Employer Obligation or Guarantee	Coverage and Eligibility Conditions	Conditions to Void or Modify the Guarantee	Corollary Employers' Policies/Programs/Buffers	Corollary Legal and Cultural Factors	Selected Experience
			poses (i.e., bankruptcy, economic difficulty). But layoffs are costly, restricted, and almost impossible, at times.		Tendency towards paternalism.	Tendency to share the work rather than seek to justify a layoff.
4. Tenure (academia)	Self-imposed moral obligation.	Teachers and some administrative staff who are considered to be "competent."	Individual dismissals only for extremely deviate conduct, e.g., poor performance. Retrenchment permitted for economic reasons.	Extremely long probationary periods (e.g., 6 years, in many cases).	Justification and rationale based on need for academic freedom.	High turnover of untenured junior persons.
5. Employment stabilization (unilaterally established by nonunion employers)	Self-imposed moral obligation, unilaterally established in nonunion situations.	All regular employees, following successful completion of probationary period.	Individual dismissals for just cause. Layoffs in extreme economic circumstances.	Hiring freezes, reduction by attrition, use of temporary employees, use of subcontractors, voluntary leaves of absence, vacation banking, early retirement, broad training,	Strong top management belief and support of employment security on paternalistic and economic-benefits grounds.	Highly motivated work force. Nonunion status.

6. Job security provisions (established by collective bargaining).	Collective bargaining agreement.	As specified in the CBA, e.g., ITV #3 and *Cincinnati Post* ("printers will be continuously employed for the remainder of their lives by the Post").	E.g., pilot programs of lifetime job security at Ford-UAW (3 plants) and GM-UAW (4 plants) for 80% of work force at these facilities.	In ITV-Post case, courts have ruled the guarantee is unambiguous and absolute.	work sharing, transfers, moving work to people, producing for inventory.
				In Ford-UAW and GM-UAW, lifetime guarantees are experimental in nature, to develop experience.	Large-scale reduction in automotive productions, leading to "concession" bargaining.
7. "Steady/secure" employment (partial and limited)	Unilateral moral commitment made in good faith but prudently hedged.	For regular full-time employees.	Dismissals for cause. Layoffs if absolutely necessary.	In Ford-UAW and GM-UAW, experiment allows, by mutual agreement, suspensions, waivers, or modifications of existing CBA.	Careful selection, broad training, long advance motive (e.g., 2 years) for layoff, severance pay, moving allowances, work sharing, inventory.

Table 1 (continued)

	Nature of Employer Obligation or Guarantee	Coverage and Eligibility Conditions	Conditions to Void or Modify the Guarantee	Corollary Employers' Policies/Programs/Buffers	Corollary Legal and Cultural Factors	Selected Experience
8. *Short-term employment guarantees (union and nonunion)*	Self-imposed moral obligations in nonunion setting (e.g., Lincoln Electric—30 hours/week for 50 weeks/year).	Employees with at least 2 years of service (no specific rate of pay is guaranteed).	Company reserves the right to terminate the guarantee, provided 6 months advance notice is given.	Employees must agree to transfer when asked and to work overtime when asked: compensation-by-piece-work incentive plan. Stock purchase plan. Employees participate as "subcontractors" and/or members of advisory board. Cash bonuses and profit sharing.		One of the oldest plans in existence—began about 1914.
	(e.g., Procter & Gamble—48 hours of regular employment guaranteed).	Limited to employees with 2 years of consecutive service.	Company may withdraw the offer.	Employee must agree to transfer when requested.		Incorporated in 1923. Revoked only once, temporarily, in 1933.
	Other examples of short-term employment guarantees often cited are: McCormick & Co., Morton Salt Co.					

	Description	Provisions	Flexibility	History/Notes
9. *Terminal employment contracts (individual)*	Individual, terminal employment contracts. Legal obligations.	Negotiated individually by managers, other professionals, actors, and athletes.		(In the period immediately following World War II, there were about 65 short-term plans in existence according to the Conference Board, some of which were employer-established, while others were agreed to in collective bargaining.
10. *Short-term income guarantees*	Annual or short-term wage/income guarantees have been established unilaterally and through collective bargaining. Examples often cited include George Hormel & Co. and the Nunn-Bush Shoe Co. Variations on this theme include the	Usually limited to regular employees with at least 6 months' service; some have required as much as 5 years' service. Right to suspend or modify if poor business conditions prevail or in the event of catastrophes and other emergencies. Financial liability in SUB limited by agreement.	Flexibility to transfer.	Many programs were started in the late 1940s as a response to the severe unemployment of the 1930s depression. Coordinated with program of unemployment insurance. Rate of survival is low. In the 1980s, the SUB programs were largely exhausted but continued to operate and in 1984 were again paying benefits.

Table 1 (continued)

Nature of Employer Obligation or Guarantee	Coverage and Eligibility Conditions	Conditions to Void or Modify the Guarantee	Corollary Employers' Policies/Programs/Buffers	Corollary Legal and Cultural Factors	Selected Experience
negotiated SUBs in the automobile and steel industry.					
11. Protection against unjust dismissal As provided by CBA, i.e., "just cause" for termination and by evolving body of law which restricts employees' right to terminate at will.	All employees, often including probationary employes.			Changing perceptions of the common-law doctrine of "employment at will."	Individuals without formal contracts now protected against "unjust dismissal."
12. Almost zero employment/income security (e.g., union construction) As negotiated with union, usually limited only to several hours of call-in pay. Employer retains and compensates craftsman for only as long as required.			Employers have right to select only those who they decide are competent.	Concept of "just cause" is beginning to be accepted in the construction industry.	Union building tradesmen have traditionally accepted this argument, wherein they work only when and for as long as required by employer decision.

Source: "Employment Stabilization," an unpublished report prepared by Lee Dyer and Associates, Ithaca, New York, 1983.

Note: CBA = collective bargaining agreement

Table 2

Comparison of Essential Short-Time Compensation Characteristics for California, Canada, and Germany

Program Characteristics	California	Canada	Germany
Eligibility			
1. Firm	Minimum 10% labor cutback; approval of union	Minimum initial workweek reduction of 20%; no less than 10% or more than 60% subsequent reduction; firm established 2 years; temporary; worker approval	Workweek reductions of at least 10% affecting no less than one-third of firm's workforce; employee approval
2. Employee	Eligible for regular UI; minimum 10% work loss; in approved work group	Eligible for regular UI; minimum 10% work loss; in approved work group	Eligible for regular UI; minimum 10% work loss; in approved work group
Benefits			
1. Replacement Rate	Same as regular UI (up to 44% depending on worker's past earnings)	Same as regular UI (up to 60% depending on worker's past earnings)	Same as regular UI (60% to 68%, depending on worker's past earnings)
2. Ceiling	$24 per day ($120 per week) in 1981; $33 per day ($166 per week) in 1983	$42 per day ($210 per week) in 1982	UI benefit 2.4 times highest U.S. ceiling in 1978

Table 2 (continued)

Program Characteristics	California	Canada	Germany
3. Post-Program Layoffs	Duration of regular UI reduced by dollar value of work-sharing benefits	No reduction of regular UI if laid off after work sharing	
Waiting Period	1 week (1 week for regular UI)	None (2 weeks for regular UI)	4 weeks
Duration and Reapplication	20 weeks; no extension; reapplication possible during next benefit year	26 weeks; 12 weeks extension; reapplication possible after period	26 weeks; possible extensions of 26 weeks and 2 years
Program Administration			
1. Contract	Claim unavoidable need; provide name and Social Security number of workers to receive benefits; union approval	Explain reason for and unavoidability of workweek reduction; provide social insurance number and other characteristics; employee approval	Evidence that workweek reductions are unavoidable and temporary; firm assumption of public fringe benefits; estimate expected duration; employee approval
2. Filing Claims	Batch claim at firm for large firms; workers file at local UI offices	Batch claim at firm by government representative	Batch claims administered in firm with government authorization

3. Benefit Payment	Benefits mailed to claimants	Benefits mailed to claimants	Employers pay benefits and are reimbursed
4. Monitoring	Review of application for eligibility compliance; review after 10 weeks	Review of application for eligibility compliance; review of complaints	Review of application for eligibility compliance; review of complaints
Funding	UI fund based on experience-rated tax of firms in accordance with past draws on fund by employees	UI fund financed by non-experience-rated taxes split unequally between firm and employees	Special UI fund financed by a 3% payroll tax split equally between firm and employees

Source: Fred Best, "Short-Time Compensation in North America: Trends and Prospects," an unpublished paper commissioned by Work in America Institute, March 1983.

Note: UI= Unemployment Insurance

Index